If Only?

TEN LIFE-ALTERING QUESTIONS
TO ASK YOURSELF

Leslie M. Chaundy, Psy.D

TRILOGY CHRISTIAN PUBLISHERS
TUSTIN, CA

Trilogy Christian Publishers
A Wholly Owned Subsidiary of Trinity Broadcasting Network
2442 Michelle Drive
Tustin, CA 92780

If Only? Ten Life-Altering Questions to Ask Yourself

Copyright © 2022 by Dr. Leslie Chaundy

Unless otherwise indicated, scripture quotations are taken from the Holy Bible, New International Version®, NIV®. Copyright © 1973, 1978, 1984, 2011 by Biblica, Inc.™ Used by permission of Zondervan. All rights reserved worldwide. www.zondervan.com. The "NIV" and "New International Version" are trademarks registered in the United States Patent and Trademark Office by Biblica, Inc.™

No part of this book may be reproduced, stored in a retrieval system, or transmitted by any means without written permission from the author. All rights reserved. Printed in the USA.

Rights Department, 2442 Michelle Drive, Tustin, CA 92780.

Trilogy Christian Publishing/TBN and colophon are trademarks of Trinity Broadcasting Network.

For information about special discounts for bulk purchases, please contact Trilogy Christian Publishing.

Trilogy Disclaimer: The views and content expressed in this book are those of the author and may not necessarily reflect the views and doctrine of Trilogy Christian Publishing or the Trinity Broadcasting Network.

Manufactured in the United States of America

10 9 8 7 6 5 4 3 2 1

Library of Congress Cataloging-in-Publication Data is available.

ISBN: 978-1-68556-362-2

E-ISBN: 978-1-68556-363-9

Dedication

This book is dedicated to my daddy: "If only" I had understood what was happening at the time, I would have gotten to know you better. But we know that God works all things together for the good of those who love Him, who are called according to His purpose (see Romans 8:28). You asked me once, "Who am I for God to save me?" Well, you sure must be something special since you were an inspiration for this book. Sometimes sacrifices are needed to save others.

This book is also, most importantly, dedicated to the Creator of all things, by whose Spirit this book was written. God, You know the purpose for everything, and I enjoy following You in faith every day, even though I don't always know where I am going. I am so glad You are all-knowing, patient, and kind. My only hope is to please You and to be a messenger of hope to others so they can get to know You before it's too late.

DEDICATION

Lastly, I would also like to thank Joshua Sprague for the thirty-day book-writing challenge, and, of course, thank you to my wonderful husband and girls for always sacrificing their time with me for the greater good.

Teach us to number our days, that we may gain a heart of wisdom.

—Psalm 90:12

Contents

Introduction vii
Chapter 1. If Only? 1
Chapter 2. Who Is This Book For? 16
Chapter 3. What in the World? 28
Chapter 4. Who Am I Really? 41
Chapter 5. Where Did I Come From? 52
Chapter 6. Why Am I Here? 64
Chapter 7. Where Am I Going? 78
Chapter 8. Which Way Is Right? 88
Chapter 9. When Is It Time? 105
Chapter 10. Whose Responsibility Is It? 116
Chapter 11. Go Thrive! 134
Chapter 12. P.S. 141
Epilogue 155

Introduction

The seal is broken. After reading this sentence, you only have ten more days to live. Yes, the countdown starts now. The clock is ticking. Are you stressed? Are you scared? Is your heart pounding? Are you thinking, *Why in the heck did I ever pick up this book? Did the author put some sort of curse on her readers, so that whoever reads her book will die in the next ten days? Is this book similar to one of those scary movies, like The Ring, where an innocent victim watches a doomed videotape and then dies several days later?*

Okay, so you are not cursed (not by me, anyway!). You are not going to die within ten days (I sure hope not!). But I hope I have created conflict in your mind and strong emotions in your body and soul. Conflict and emotions get people to read books, watch movies, and think about things. They get your attention. That is my true intention. I want to get your attention! Our brains have too many things to think about. We are pulled in too many directions. We don't know what should be our

INTRODUCTION

priority. And we don't know what we don't know. Are you confused yet? Let me explain a bit more.

The purpose of this book is to get you to think about greater things. Things that, if you only had ten days to live, you would most likely focus on. Some of you may think about these things already on a daily basis. Some of you may only think about these things on an occasional basis. Some of you may never think of these things at all because you don't have time. Some of you have no intention of ever thinking about these things at any great length at all. Lastly, some of you may think these are stupid questions. But I do have "for real" bad news for you—and this is a not a joke or a lie. There is a seal that was broken. That seal was broken the day you were born. The countdown began, my friend. The clock was put into motion. Now, I do not know if you will live seventy more years, seven more months, or seven more days. But I do know *as an absolute fact* is that we all have a limited time left on this earth. We will all die—myself included. The unfortunate thing is, we all think we have a lot of time left, so we don't prioritize our time. I mean, we prioritize our daily functions at work, our duties at home, and school activities. But what I am talking about is the real meaning of life. These are the biggest questions you should be asking yourself. Don't worry, we will get to these questions in due time.

I wanted to put this out there. I know some of the questions or activities in this book might seem silly on the surface. For some of you, the questions might seem too big or massive to think about at all. If you concentrate on them for any length of time, you might feel your brain will explode. Some of you might feel like some of these questions don't have any definite answers. You question the importance about thinking about them at all. Some of you don't care, and some of you just don't know what you don't know.

Let me explain it this way. In the wake of COVID-19, my eighteen-year-old daughter was stuck at home and could not go away to college. She took it well because she didn't know what she was missing and what college life entailed. I was more upset than she was because I have been to college and experienced all the fun. I know what she is missing out on: College is a lot of fun; it was one of the best experiences of my life. But my daughter doesn't know what she doesn't know.

We, too, may be missing out on so much more if we do not think about life and what happens afterward. We could be missing the boat if we do not ask the big questions to find out more about things we don't know or care about. For many of us, it will simply be too late. You don't want to have to live with regret and disappointment over any missed opportunity.

So, that is why I want you to think, imagine, and believe with all your heart and soul, right now, that you only have ten days to live. Meditate on these things—

INTRODUCTION

not to scare yourself, but to motivate yourself to think about the things that matter most. Ask the questions you should be asking if you truly only had ten days to live. Think of it as a challenge, a ten-day challenge. I will help you. I will guide you on this existential journey by giving you ten days of important things to think about. The next ten chapters contain a series of questions to ask yourself. Each day, I will discuss one of the important ten questions. Your task is to make this a priority. Take quality time to read the chapter and think about the questions at length throughout the day. It is best to start thinking of them in the morning. Then think about these things throughout the day as though you *really* only have a few more days left on this earth. I would hope you would give these questions more than a few minutes a day. I know we all have the constraints of jobs, families, activities, and multiple responsibilities. Although, I am sure if you only had ten days to live, these would be all-consuming questions in your head. Some of you may have already been told you only have a limited time left on earth, or you know someone who has. Why do we wait until these times to think about such things?

 I have provided you space in this book after each chapter for you to journal your personal thoughts and reflections each day. This is a place for you to write down your observations and any further questions. Try to learn about the things you don't know. Try to complete the activities and answer the following questions each day. This book should give you more questions than answers. At the end of the book, you should want to search for more. That is the bad news. If this book works correctly, you may have more questions than you started out with, but that is good. That is the true intention behind this book. It is to inspire you to seek out truth. We all question on some level the reason for our existence and what happens afterward. Let the fear of you dying in ten days fuel that questioning. The great King Solomon stated that the "fear of the LORD" is often the beginning of wisdom and knowledge (see Proverbs 1:7). Most of us don't seek truth for ourselves; we take or share someone else's version. Let the fear of death help you seek the truth for yourself. Seek and you shall find.

I do want to provide a disclaimer here. My intention is not to cause you undue anxiety or fear that puts you into a state of panic. I almost named this book *Seal Broken* or *Countdown Starts Now*. My friend said that she didn't like those titles because they were too anxiety-producing. But a little anxiety can be good. If you didn't have a little bit of anxiety, you wouldn't have opened your books in school to study for the tests. You wouldn't have performed well in sports, or been successful in your job if you did not prepare. Yet, the exact opposite is also true. If you have too much anxiety, you will freeze

INTRODUCTION

up and feel paralyzed during the test, run away, or fight. My hope is that your anxiety level will be just right, so that you do not feel frozen with fear or put this book down and run away. There is good news to be found in this book. Unless you are actually having a panic attack when you think about dying, then this book is not for you. However, if you are experiencing such severe anxiety, then I do have to ask this question: What are you so afraid of? Maybe you should keep reading so that you will not be so fearful in the future. Expose yourself to some of these scary questions. (That is one of the treatments for anxiety.) Hiding away and avoiding the question only makes the anxiety grow, like a virus on a computer. Face your fears. In my work as a psychologist, I have helped many people who had brushes with death in car accidents, who then never want to drive again. They come to me distressed, their anxiety so great that they can't even leave their home. They come to me to help them get their lives back. I tell them that they have to get back in the driver's seat. I tell them they have to sit in it for a few days and then slowly start to drive again, even if it's only down the block. They may resist, but those who follow those recommendations get better. They eventually drive again. The fear goes away. Sure, a small amount of fear is always there. It's like a tiny voice in the back of their head, but it isn't so big that it controls them. They control it. So, with that being said, take back control of your life! Face your fears. Face your demons. Let's get started.

Wait, I almost forgot about the other side of anxiety! It can also cause adrenaline to kick in, and some people don't take "flight"—instead they "fight." Again, this is not my intention for you. My intention is only to get you to open your mind and think about some possibilities. I just finished binge-watching *Grey's Anatomy*. In one of the episodes, Dr. Karev came home and found a coworker bent over his girlfriend. He started throwing punches before the guy could explain that his girlfriend was intoxicated, and he was just putting her to bed. Dr. Karev went into "fight" mode. That cost him a long unnecessary road of stress and heartache with the threat of prison over his head. If he had just waited and listened for a few minutes, he could have avoided a lot of undue stress. The same is true for those people out there who already feel angry with me. Don't throw the punches yet. Give me some time to explain. Hear the whole story. Okay, so now, without further ado, let's get started. What are some of these *very important questions?*

CHAPTER 1

If Only?

I heard the door open—and then the footsteps. One by one, they descended the old wooden steps, each one of them squeaking. It seemed like an eternity, but I knew. I knew what it meant. It was done. It was over. She was home. I waited for the words. I waited with my heart thumping a million beats a minute in my chest. *Say the words—just say the words,* my mind screamed in anticipation. The few seconds it took her to come down the steps felt like forever. My breath became shallow. She was hesitating. I knew she didn't want to tell us. Finally, after a long, torturous pause, the words came. Her eyes were wet with tears, worried about the impact her words would have on her two children forever. The weight of those words. Those two dreaded words, "Daddy died." There it was... I needed a few minutes to process the weight of that sentence. "Daddy died, Daddy died, Daddy died." Daddy was really gone? What did that even mean? I sat in silence. My mind was trying to wrap my head around those insane thoughts and the meaning of those two crazy words. My brother's voice brought me out of my stupor. "Can I call a friend?" I thought, *What kind of question was that? REALLY? That is all you've got to say?* Now my mind was stuck on processing those words. But after a minute, as the words soaked in, the idea didn't seem so bad. Okay, yes, let's call our friends and let them know. I know it seemed like a strange comment at the time. But it also seemed like a good idea to get ourselves out of the awkward silence and situation. Off we went to call our friends. The actual thought of anything real faded away. The business of the funeral and family and friends visiting kept us busy.

I was thirteen. A teenager. I was supposed to be going out with friends and having fun. I was supposed to be enjoying life and thinking of stupid and meaningless things like, *What am I going to wear to school tomorrow?* I actually do remember the same night, right before he died, being very worried about that silly problem. Death was a big question for such a little mind. The true meaning of life and death at age thirteen was incomprehensible. I just didn't know what I didn't know. Most people don't have to think about those questions until much later in life, but here I was. I have to be honest with you, I didn't think much more about it. I probably thought of that question for about two minutes that night. After that, I put it on the back burner. I felt depleted. I had

IF ONLY?

just spent the last three years thinking about cancer. I had seen my father go from a 350-pound man to something unrecognizable. At the end of his battle with cancer, he looked more like a prisoner of war than my dad. I was done. I didn't want to hear another word about it. I didn't want to think about it. I didn't want to talk about it. Thinking back, it wasn't a question I had the capacity to think about, or maybe no one ever made me think about it. My mind was more worried about boys, friends, and drama at school. You know—the stuff that was in front of me. The stuff I can see. The stuff that seemed to matter at the time.

I went on the next several years not ever really thinking about it. I just went about life. I mean, I missed him. He was always in my mind at things like graduation or milestone events. I would think, "I wish Dad was here," but like the wind, the light touch of those feelings would flow through my body and then would be gone without a trace. No sense chasing the wind, right? I believed that he was somewhere else, like maybe at a vacation house or on a temporary move. I would see him one day. I put it out of my mind. I believed without question like a child. I was a good kid. I didn't question. My mom told me where he was. He was in heaven. When you are a child, you think your parents are all-knowing. I didn't think about it. They told me where he was, and I believed. I would see him again, and that was that. Life went on. It had to. We all went on, too. I loved him. But I didn't cry. I am not sure why... I had a childlike faith, I guess. But I didn't cry. I remember everyone telling me it was okay to cry. But I didn't need to. I didn't want to. What was there to cry about? I would see him again. He was in some distant land that I didn't think much about. It was temporary. I had such an amazing faith.

I know what you may be thinking. Yes, it's childlike to have faith. But that's not where my story ended. It wasn't until many, many years later that I would question. I would question life. My life had taken on a life of its own, and I followed it. Many people don't know this, but I went into the mental health field because of a hospice social worker I had encountered. It was not because that social worker was great. It was they were a terrible, horrible social worker—or so I thought at the time. I was in the seventh grade. I had skipped the last period of that day, which was baton practice. I was in the bathroom with a bunch of girls who had also skipped practice. My entire life up until that point, I had never skipped anything. Yet I remember that day very well because the call came on the loudspeaker—it seems like it was yesterday. Do you remember that one embarrassing experience when you were thirteen, and you don't want any attention brought to yourself, especially one that blares throughout the whole school that you are in trouble? "Leslie Schlegel, please report to the high school office. Leslie Schlegel, please report to the high school office." I remember my best friend finding it hysterical. "Darn it. They caught me! Man, what is in store for me? Ugh!" I walked the walk of shame to the principal's office, expecting the worst. The principal had never called me to the office before. I wasn't sure what to expect. But to my surprise, my grandparents were there. Relief came flooding over me when I saw them. I knew they were there to pick me up and take me to the hospital. I had been there many times before. "Whew, got out of that one!" I thought. I thanked God in the car the whole way to the hospital. I had been rescued from the wrath of being discovered skipping practice, and I was grateful. I don't think they ever did find out I was missing in baton that day.

When we got to the hospital, we were told someone wanted to meet with us. We walked to the waiting room alone and sat down on the couch, me and my ten-year-old brother next to me. And there she was, the dreaded hospice worker. At the time, I didn't even know what the word hospice meant. Weirdly enough, although my father had known he was dying for several months, we had never met with her until that day, most likely because he was not sent home to die. After the briefest introduction ever, she asked the question, "Are you ready to let your father go?" What the heck was she talking about? Go where? She asked the question a second time. What the heck was she talking about? I looked at my brother, and he looked at me. We truly had no idea what she was talking about. We felt like we only had the choice to say yes, not sure what exactly we were agreeing to. After that two-minute conversation, we all got up and followed her out of the room. Meanwhile, my brother and I were looking at each other and making goofy faces. We were laughing and thinking, "Who the heck is this chick?" She was so weird and awkward, and she made us feel awkward. Honestly, she might have said other stuff too. Perhaps we were too young to understand. Maybe we had heard it before, and it was just redundant. Again, we don't know what we don't know. Whatever the reason, in our minds she was weird. The whole thing was weird.

The next thing we knew, we were standing next to our father's bedside. They told us to say the words over him, "I am ready to let him go." Let him go where, I still didn't know. But I wanted this woman to go away, so I said the words, not thinking too much of them.

I walked out of my father's hospital room not much later, glancing back. His eyes were following me as he lay there, so thin with a sunken-in face. That was the last time I ever saw him. I only glanced back. If only I had known that was the last time I would see him, I would have given him a bigger hug. If I had been older, wiser, more mature, and more insightful, I would have said something or asked him something. Something more. But I didn't think about it. How could I? I was only thirteen. My brain could not process what was going on. I am sure they told us, but I didn't know what I didn't know. Maybe I was more immature than others. That's most likely the case. But I just didn't really think about what was happening. I am not sure why. My brain wasn't there yet. Developmentally, I just wasn't there.

And yet, that day changed the course of my life. I went on to become a social worker and psychologist, and I went on to own two private mental health practices. I was a good person. I knew I was going to see my father again one day. I was doing great things. I was helping people. That's what I was expected to do, right? I was making lemonade out of those lemons. I wanted to help kids who were going through the same experiences of grief and loss. I would see my father again, because good people went to heaven. Right? So, I thought, until one day I was sitting in a church pew, and the pastor, I still remember, brought out a very large ladder. Where do you fall on this ladder, in terms of being a good person? he asked. Well, I was no Mother Teresa, for sure; she was at the top. But I wasn't a mass murder either, so I wasn't at the bottom. But hey, I was a pretty good person. I had dedicated my life to helping people. I was pretty proud of myself. I thought I was in the third or fourth ring from the top, maybe?

As I gloated to myself with self-satisfaction, my bubble was burst. My pastor blurted out, "You don't get to heaven that way. It's only if you believe." I thought, "WHAT? Are you telling me I just wasted more than fifteen years of my life and at least seven years of post–high school education doing something that was difficult for me?" (I was shy and had anxiety about being around people, and I had always pushed myself to do it.) Now I discovered that everything I had worked so hard for was a lie—all for nothing? "ARE YOU KIDDING ME?"

The rules had changed. I would never see my father in heaven, then? For the first time ever, I wasn't sure what I believed. It was most likely the first time I had ever thought about it "for real." I had always believed in God because other people told me to. I wanted to see my father again someday, and so it wasn't a choice. It just was. But what was I going to do now?

I went home that night and wrote my pastor a two- or three-page letter, sobbing as I penned the words. "I don't think I believe in God. I don't think I am going to heaven." That was difficult for me! I was about thirty years old. I was coming to the questions late. Better late than never, I guess. But how had I never considered this question before? How could I get to this age without ever "really" thinking about it? How could I be thirty and never really have "thought" about what all of this was for? About what happens after we die? If people would ask, I would say, of course, I was a Christian. But did I even know what that meant? Apparently not. I couldn't, like most people, even answer the most basic questions of what that meant.

That day started my quest for truth.

So, that is my story. What is yours? We all have a journey. Some of you may be wondering what is the point of me telling you "my story"? What does that have to do with anything? I have learned two very important things through my experience, and I want to share them with you. There are two themes throughout this book that would be important to you if you knew you were going to die in ten days. Like a mirror or a reflection on a pond, there are two sides: the physical and the mirrored image. Both are important parts of the big, beautiful picture. It is the same if you were dying in ten days. You should be concerned about the physical place you will be going as well as the reflection that you will leave behind here.

Let's start with the reflection. People generally don't want to leave the earth, especially if they have loved ones. So, the first big question that you should be asking yourself, if you only have ten days left on this earth to live, is, "If only…" If only you would have known you would be gone in ten days, what would you have done differently? This is one of the questions you must ask yourself to avoid regret. In my story, my regret was that

I didn't say good-bye to my dad like it was the last time I would see him. But I didn't know what I didn't know at the time. Oh, let's be clear: They told me. But I didn't understand. My mind was not there yet. So, that is one question I want you to ask yourself every day throughout this challenge: If only...? If you only knew you had ten days left, what would you do differently?

For example, as I was literally typing the words for this book, my younger daughter came to me and asked me to take her to the store. I was agitated because she was imposing upon my time. "Ugh! right now?" I exclaimed, not happy at the unexpected interruption. I was certainly not living like someone who thought they only had ten days left to live. Because if I did, I would have spent that time with her and I wouldn't have been so agitated. If I had used the "if only" question, I would have relished that time with her. I would have appreciated those few stolen last minutes together and taken her to the store without hesitation. I would have made her a priority. That is the "if only" question.

That should be a question for you every day. You should think about how you reflect upon others and how you want to be reflected upon when you leave this world. But to have reflection, you need light. Reflect the light. Always remember that.

Now, I realize that if we lived as though we only had ten days to live every day, we wouldn't get any work done. There are many tedious things that we need to do throughout each day, such as cooking, cleaning, shopping, and of course, working. Most of us, if we felt well but we knew we only had ten days left, would be off to a tropical island to spend our last days feasting with family and friends. I understand that. Remember, this is only a challenge to get you thinking, not to actually give you a vacation from work for ten days. (Well, what the heck, you could take a vacation if you wanted to!) Remember, my intention is to help you reflect on, at the end of the day, what you would have done differently. If you knew you would be gone in ten days, how would others remember you? My hope is to help you learn to prioritize a little bit better and focus more on the things that matter in the end. That alone can help us in finding meaning, understanding, and purpose in the world.

But that is only the first question. The reflection question is only one side of the equation. But what's on the other side? That is the other theme I want you to think about. What is on the other side of this lifetime? On all journeys, we come to a crossroads, as the one above in my story. In my story, I faced the crossroads of what I believe. We all come to a place and time when we have to make decisions—decisions that could ultimately impact our future. If you had ten days left to live, that would put you at a crossroads. You would start thinking more about the future after death, or the lack of it. Is not eternity, and where you will spend it, one of the biggest questions of your life?

Crossroads on any journey are scary because we often feel lost or confused. We don't know which way to turn or which way is the correct way to go. We avoid making the decisions, or we don't have time to search for the answers. We think we have lots of time left. We can all agree that there are definitely times in our life when we are confused. We feel lost, broken down, and unsure of which way to go. But we all have a final destination that we want to get to. Whether it be home, or a better place than what we perceive to be our home, we want to get to the final destination. Some of us may like the challenge of the journey. Others may want to sit down and cry, feeling as though you have been left alone in the middle of this dark, scary world. You think no one cares about you or is searching for you. Some people may not feel lost or believe they are lost at all. I mean, you don't know what you don't know.

However, the timer is almost up. You only have ten more days to live. Where will your next destination be? You, my friend, have ten days left until you cross out of this world. The alarm will go off shortly. You have to make a turn. You have to make a decision. Perhaps you are okay with remaining in this position forever, buried in the earth for eternity, or worst-case scenario, spending forever in a far more horrible place than this. Do you want to take the chance? Again, most of us don't care, because we are not in a position of dying soon. But I will ask you again, if you only have ten days left, would you start thinking about it then? You would want to be prepared for what's next—if there is anything—right?

It reminds me of the movie *Hunger Games*, or *Maze Runner*. We are trapped in a dome or a dimension or a maze or something that we can't get out of. It's like some cruel person has put us there and our very survival depends on our timely escape. We have to figure out how the maze works or find the small entrance to get out. There is too much information to navigate through. You have to make a decision to turn left or right. Your life and safety depend on it. There are too many choices. But imagine, you will only see your family again if you turn in the right direction. I know it's difficult, but try really hard to imagine that you are stuck. For some of you, I know you don't have to imagine it. The struggle is real. But whether it feels real or not, think of it as a metaphor for your life. We are stuck here. Many of us are not sure where, why, or what the point is. But in order to get out safely, while not completely unscathed, we have to ask the big questions in life. What are these big questions? Well, one is, how can we know if there is anything more after this life? We will take this one step at a time and break it down in the next chapters. But for now, work on your self-reflection questions for today.

Self-Reflection Questions

1. What is one thing that stood out to you in the reading?

2. What did you learn from it?

3. Have you ever thought about death?

4. Does the thought of dying scare you? Why or why not?

5. Have you ever lost anyone close to you?

6. Have you ever thought of life after death?

7. What would you like to learn more about?

8. How can you learn more about it?

IF ONLY?

9. How would others reflect on you and your life?

10. What is one thing you would you have done differently today "if only" you had known you would be gone in ten days?

CHAPTER 2

Who Is This Book For?

Let's imagine for a few minutes you are with your family on vacation in Brazil. You are at the hotel, and you all decide to take a guided tour to visit the great Amazon rain forest. You are super-excited. You hop on the tour bus and sit back and relax. You daydream about all the exciting things you will see. You can't wait to see all the exotic birds, animals, and reptiles. Even the giant, disgusting insects seem fascinating to you at this point. Your tour bus arrives at the entrance of where the great forest begins. Once you go in, there is no looking back. You are glad you have a guide. But everything is so amazing. It's easy to wander away and take your eyes off the guide. I mean, come on, there are adorable monkeys out there! You walk around in wonder and amazement. Everything is so new and exciting.

Then, all of a sudden, you are actually looking at it! You cannot believe your eyes. You have seen pictures of them, but never, ever before have you been this close to one. You gasp as a giant anaconda slithers across the grass. An ANACONDA! I mean, oh my goodness, what if it eats you whole? I mean, there are pictures of that happening on the internet. You are scared to death, but someone on the bus told you that these creatures rarely actually attack humans. Those stories and pictures are all fabricated. They told you anacondas only attack when provoked, and so, with great excitement, you reach for your phone. This is so exciting. I mean, seriously, this is a picture-worthy moment. You can't wait to show all your friends. You bend over and position yourself just far enough away from this creature that you can see its beauty but not get hurt, and then…

You're running. Running full-force. You are not sure what happened, but you got spooked. You took off. You lost your grounding. You ran. Why you didn't run toward your family or toward the tour guide, you simply don't know. You just took off. It was fight or flight. As you slow down, you realize you have entered the thick of things. Suddenly you stop, mostly because you are getting tangled up in the mess of thick plants and weeds. You can't see anything in front of you. And for the first time ever, you realize you are lost. You didn't go far. But nevertheless, you are lost. So, what should you do?

The first thing to do in any situation is not panic. You have been running. Take a minute. Breathe. Slow your brain down so you can think logically. Assess your surroundings. You look around, but nothing looks familiar. You are definitely lost. There is no one around. You call out. No one answers. *Darn it. They can't hear me. They can't see me. I am all alone.* You start to panic. *Maybe they are searching for me? Maybe they don't even know I am missing? Maybe they don't even care about me? Maybe they are dead? Okay, it doesn't matter. I cannot depend on them. They are not here right now. It's up to me to get me out of this mess if I want to see my family again.*

Okay, so what do you do next? Think. Think. Think. Are there any markers, a map, or directions or something? You remember the gift shop had lots of guides and maps, too many to choose from. You remember your guide gave you one, so you pull it out and glance at it. It doesn't make any sense, and it's too long and confusing. You don't understand the language in which the map was written. There are also multiple maps within maps on the page with various paths. You are not even sure what exact part of the jungle you are in or which one is correct. You put the map back in your pocket. *Boy, was that unhelpful. It's too scary out here to stare at a map,* you think. *I have to keep moving. There is no time to stop and figure out that map.*

You start walking, trying to make your way through the thick trees and overgrowth. You just get farther away. You're getting more worried. More time is passing. You realize you are getting farther away from the others, not closer. You keep trying to do it alone. Okay, so now what do you do? What are some of the questions you would need to ask yourself in order to get out of the rain forest safely?

These are some of the same questions we need to ask ourselves in this world when we feel lost. Do you want to get safely home? I know I may have gone off on a tangent with the jungle scenario, but let's bring it back home. If you had ten days to live (actually nine, now), that would be the first and foremost question you should ask yourself: Are you lost?

If you were lost in a jungle, at some point, I imagine you would be screaming and cursing at God or the universe. You would feel like some cruel twist of fate happened, that you landed in the middle of the Amazon rain forest alone, when you thought you were taking a special and memorable vacation. We scream out so the Creator of the universe can hear our anger and disappointment, our idea that life wasn't supposed to be this way. You didn't sign up for this. You signed up for the AAA tour package. Not this! Not this jungle. Not this life.

This book is for people like you. It's for people who are at the point in their lives where they are questioning life or feeling lost in this world. Wondering what the point of it is. Feeling like life has no meaning. No purpose. Feeling like life is just one big hamster wheel

WHO IS THIS BOOK FOR?

and you can't get off, or for some of you, wondering where you are going when you do get off. Wondering if there is anything more outside this hamster wheel. Wondering if there is anything beyond this, spinning planet we call earth that is hurtling across the universe. Is this book for you? This is the number-one question you should ask yourself. Do you care? I mean, seriously, do you care? Think of this first question as the basis for everything else in this book. Why read the rest of this book if you don't care about that question?

I am not trying to be a jerk here, but lots of people say they care. But then, do they really think about it for any significant length of time? Have you actually taken the time to research it and plan what might happen after you die? Think about this next question. Did you care more about planning your last vacation than planning or thinking about what happens next after you die? I don't mean planning a funeral. If you really had only nine more days to live, would you care more about that question? Do you care about where you may be going, or about seeing your deceased family members and loved ones again? Do you want to get safely home? Do you want to go to a better place? What if there really is a worse place than this? Do you feel lost in this world?

I know you may have briefly thought about the meaning of life and an afterlife, maybe while talking with people over dinner. Or maybe even in more depth during philosophical conversations with family and friends. But have you gone beyond that to search for answers? Some of you may have, and that is good. Some of you may feel that you already have the map, that you can read it and understand it, and that you already have the directions—and that is good. Finding the right map and the right directions will determine how long and hard your road will be.

Going back to the jungle scenario, wouldn't it be upsetting if you spent two weeks in the jungle, only to be told when they found you that you had the directions all along. The tour guide would say, "Why didn't you use my map and follow the path?"

You would say, "It was too hard to read, and I didn't have the time. I was too busy running away from everything. It was hard work getting through the jungle! And besides, there were too many maps to decide from."

Your tour guide would make you look at the map again, and when you flip it over, you realize that if you had just taken the time to examine it more closely, you would have seen the map right there in your own language. You just didn't take the time or make the effort. Instead, you took the long way.

In your life, you may feel you are not lost at all. This reminds me of Plato's "allegory of the cave." Prisoners who were forced to live in a cave, chained to a wall, saw shadows, which became their reality. They didn't know what was truly on the outside of the cave, nor did they understand that what they saw was not an accurate representation of the real world. They were trapped in their reality. In much the same way, we are trapped in the reality of our own world. Some of us don't know we are trapped, or we don't feel trapped at all. Remember: You don't know what you don't know. The cave analogy points to a higher truth: that other levels of reality do exist, and that education is important in gaining awareness of it. Science and math are a higher form of reality, yet even above that, there exists something higher. We don't know what we don't know! Science and math are only the beginning to full understanding, not the end.

Some people take science as fact, when in fact, scientists don't even know what they don't know yet. Human beings are learning and finding out new things every day. That is not to say that science is bad. It's just that we don't know what we don't know yet. In science, it is often the search that is most important. Many of us don't search or question whether there is anything beyond this life. We blindly take what we are given from experts who believe they know everything there is to know. But right now, they "just know what they know." Science is good. However, it is still only one layer of reality we experience before we move to the next. I think people forget that fact.

Whether you feel lost or not, I will ask the question again: Is this book for you? That is your question for today. Do you really care—and why? If you care, there are two ways to find your way home when you are lost and don't know where you are going. There is the easy way, and there is the hard way. But first of all, you have to figure out if you are lost and whether or not you care that you are. Because if you don't believe you are lost or care that you are, then what motivation is there for you to get safely home? None.

All of us may think about life on some level every day. But this book is for those who want to take more time to think and go more in depth. I am talking third-level depth (remember the allegory of the cave). This book is for those who want to open their minds to consider their human existence: Why are we here, where did we come from, where are we going, and how can we best get there? Are these not questions worth thinking about? I believe that they are, especially if we are going to die soon. Isn't it worth spending just a few minutes a day pondering our lives?

This book is a starting place for you to examine some of those questions. I don't have all the answers. I am not the ultimate tour guide. I can be a helper, but I am not the ultimate guide. I can share with you some of the questions to consider, but you have to take the next step. You have to choose. Are you excited? Are you skeptical?

WHO IS THIS BOOK FOR?

Are you hopeful, or are you pessimistic that this will be just another book with a disappointing end? I hope not, but I can promise you I will at least get you thinking and spark your curiosity about these big questions—the biggest questions of your life. There are no other questions like it—especially if you are going to die in nine days!

You may think we all get to that point in our lives when we start asking questions. So, how is this book different from others? This book is a starting place—a place to start thinking about the true meaning of life. That is the whole purpose of this book: to get you thinking and becoming more curious about the world. We all go to school and learn things we often don't care about at the time, and then a majority of us forget most of what we learned in school. For most people, school is a task, a nuisance, something to do so we can get some type of diploma. Most of us are too immature to understand the reason for school and appreciate it at the time, especially in our younger years. Some of us enjoy learning, and we go on to college. But even then, depending on our maturity, college can be just one big assignment. The biggest question becomes, What do I have to do to get my degree and then get a good job in the field of my choice?

We often skip over the big questions. I mean, why not? They are unanswerable, right? We can't solve these questions, so it's better not to think about them.

It's a waste of time at best. Yes, it may be true that we don't know the answers to these big questions. But that doesn't mean they are not worth a few minutes of our time every day.

So again, I do not profess to know all the answers. I am only a helper, the tour guide. I am trying to guide you to the right place and help you to think about the possibilities. The choice is yours. God has given each of us free will. I am only going to nudge you to think about the right questions, not half-heartedly, but in depth. I am going to give you exercises every day to open your mind, to open your curiosity. Try to spend at least fifteen to twenty minutes each day considering these questions. What is fifteen minutes of your life if it gives it more meaning? Isn't your future worth it? What do you have to lose? Finding meaning and purpose adds peace to your life. Research says that if you have meaning, purpose, and peace in your life, anxiety and depression will decrease and your physical health will improve. Open your eyes and see. Let's begin the real journey! As my sweet college roommate would always say, "Buckle up, my friend. Let's tackle this mountain together!"

Self-Reflection Questions

1. Is this book for you?

2. Do you care about what happens to you after you die? Why or why not?

3. Do you ever feel lost in this world? Why or why not?

4. Would you like to spend more time to thinking about these important questions?

5. What one thing stood out for you in the reading today?

6. What did you learn from it?

7. What would you like to learn more about?

IF ONLY?

8. How can you learn more?

9. What are some more questions that you would have if you knew you were going to die in nine days?

10. Now for the "if only" question: What would you have done differently today if you had known you'd be gone in nine days?

CHAPTER 3

What in the World?

I'm a busy person. I own two businesses with almost twenty clinicians. I have two girls, a husband, and older parents who were recently in the process of a move and have numerous health issues. Not to mention all the tasks of daily life. I get it. I get the busyness of life. It whisks you away, and before you know it, years seem like months, months seem like days, and days seem like moments. The Bible tells us that one day is like a thousand years to God (see 2 Peter 3:8). I wish! I swear, time is moving faster and faster the older I get.

I remember when my girls were little, before they ever knew the concept of time. When it got dark, we would tell them it was time for bed. It was about 5:30 or 6 p.m. They didn't realize it was actually a few hours before bedtime, but the darkness outside clouded their sense of time. It was great. It didn't matter if we put them to bed at 6 p.m. or 8 p.m., they would sleep the same amount of time. Sometimes I wonder if God is spinning the earth faster, and we just don't know it.

Well, more on the concept of time later, but for now I wanted to get back to the task at hand. My thoughts here on time has to do with the fact that we are so busy, we don't often look around us.

That certainly would be important if we were stuck in a jungle. It would be important to assess our surroundings. We are stuck here on the earth. Where exactly are we, and what do our surroundings tell us?

For example, when is the last time that you went outside, took a walk, and looked at the bark on the trees around you? I know that is a completely strange question. I remember a few months ago, I made a promise to myself that I would get outside and take more walks. I walked to the bottom of my property, which is at the bottom of a hill. There is a bridge at the bottom that takes you across a stream to another piece of land we call the "jungle." It sounds like a jungle with all the birds and crickets chirping back there in the summer. It's about an acre or two of many trees and briars, and it is nearly impossible to walk through. When my husband cleared a small patch across the bridge, he needed a machete to do so.

One day, when I was walking across the bridge to the other side, I noticed a little box sitting in the middle of the overgrown part of the woods. It was about a hundred yards away. I wondered what was in the box. I had never seen it there before. I had lived in my house for almost twenty years at that point, but I had only ever been on that side of the stream maybe five times. My curiosity got the best of me that day, and I attempted to go into the "jungle" to look inside the box. It was not easily accessible. But I went anyway, determined to see what was in it. I found my way over to it, scraping the side of my face on multiple tree branches. I had tiny scars to document my bravery in getting to the other side. I did it! I was so proud of myself—especially since I have the biggest phobia of ticks. But I did it! To my surprise and dissatisfaction, there was nothing in the box. I was disheartened. Something had been leading me over to it. And then nothing.

Well, while I was there, I decided to open my eyes a little more. And to my surprise, I felt like a kid again. Everything seemed so new and exciting. I remember looking at the bark of a tree and remembering sixth-grade camp. That was the last time I think I'd ever really looked at the bark of a tree. I remember in sixth-grade camp looking for moss on a tree. Had I not looked at a tree since then? I must have, right? But I don't think so. In fact, I don't think I have really looked at a tree my entire adult life. Not really. I've glanced at trees, yes. Seen them with my eyes, yes. But to really look at a tree and truly see it? No. Now, maybe if I was traveling to see the great sequoias, I would have opened my eyes and really looked at them. But for the most part, I look at trees like an adult, not like a child—with wonder and questions. I know we learned all about trees and flowers in school. I have a vague knowledge of all that. Man, do I wish I could go back to school now, when I actually care about this stuff...about the clouds, trees, animals, and bugs.

I swore that day that *every day* I would get out, walk around, and spend time with God and His creation. And guess what? I haven't been down there since. That is the truth. Time is a thief. It takes me away. It takes everyone away from enjoying the little things. My mom told me that when my father was dying, he said he'd never taken the time to enjoy the birds. He only took the time when he knew he was going to die. Some of you may study the birds, or take walks on a daily basis, or enjoy the beauty of the sunrise on a consistent basis. That is excellent. But you are the exception.

Most of us look at the scenery during times of vacation or on the off chance that we see something interesting. Then we ponder it for a few minutes and then go on with our busy lives. How easily we forget! I want to you to look around and really see the world around you, not because you have to, but because you want to. And not with your eyes, but with your soul. I want you be a child again. Full of wonder and grace. Questioning, like a child. Remember when you drove your parents crazy, questioning every little thing because everything was new? Maybe you have kids who do that now.

WHAT IN THE WORLD?

Imagine you are on a quest. Don't believe what others tell you, but search for the answers yourself. To begin the search, you need to open your eyes. I want you to get up and go outside. Go to the nearest tree and look at the bark. Notice its color, its texture, its beauty despite its ugliness. Run your hands across it. It's just a tree, but yet how much more can a simple thing mean when you really look at it and think about it. Think about the purpose of a tree. It is here to serve you. It gives you shelter. It gives paper to write on. It gives you oxygen. It gives you food. It gives you fruit. It gives you nuts. Maybe it just gives you beauty. Think about that tree that you probably pass every day and never think about. The tree you might have climbed on as a little kid. Think about it. Why is it here, where did it come from, and what happens after it dies? If you live in the north, think about the beauty of the four seasons. You can watch the trees transform from buds and flowers, to vibrant green leaves, to spectacular fall colors, and end up as dead stick branches. But those are more questions for later. For now, I just want you really look around at the world and notice it. Look at the piece of fruit the tree bears. How amazing and different each fruit is. They have different colors, shapes, textures, and tastes. Run your hand over them and notice the differences. Taste them. How different and unique they all are! There are the same, but yet they cannot be compared. I know you learned

IF ONLY?

all about trees and fruits in elementary school, and perhaps you can remember what you studied. But for now, I just want you to notice it and enjoy it. Pay attention to the design of it. Think about how each one was created so different and unique. They were created just to serve you. Think about how they have seeds. Isn't it amazing that each seed produces another fruit? If you truly think about these things for five minutes, it will astonish you. How great and good and well-designed everything is. But we miss it. We miss it when we don't think about it. We learn about it, but we don't think about and meditate on such things. We try to meditate inwardly and become one with the universe, but we don't look around to see it for what it truly is. Could these amazing things have just come from nothing? Just arrived here perfect? Arrived here in a perfect assortment of different shapes and different colors? Or were they put here for a purpose? Yes, I know the science of fruit and trees. Science is good, it helps us understand, but just for a minute think of how perfect it is. Think of what a magnificent creation a tree is. Was it created? I know I can't answer that for you. All I ask is you think on it. Think more than the second it takes to walk past the tree. Meditate on it.

I want you to think of one more thing. If the tree is created for us for shelter and food, should we be worshiping the tree or the One who created it? My daughter Bella is an artist. She often paints or draws beautiful things. She brings them to me, and I am in awe at the beauty of the things she creates. But even more so, I am amazed at *her*. How do her hands craft such wonderful things? I love the pictures she makes, but more than my amazement at the picture is the awe I have in her, at how she could create such beautiful things. How she could take nothing and make it something. How sad she would be if I didn't give her credit. How sad if I hung her picture up and worshiped the picture without ever mentioning that she was the creator of the masterpiece. How hurt would she be? I would never do that to her. She is special. She is deserving of the praise of her work. I don't know if you believe in God or not. Maybe not. And that's okay. I don't want to jam religion down your throat. We are just contemplating on life. That is the only purpose of this book. I just want you to look around and pretend that you have eight more days now to do that. Yes, the countdown is at eight now! Give me eight more days. Pretend with all your heart that in eight more days, you will exist no more. What things would you notice that maybe you didn't notice before? What more questions would you have about the things you see and can smell, touch, taste, and hear? What would you take notice of? Could all of this just have arrived here for nothing? Out of nowhere? Just magically appeared? A banana just appeared out of nothing, or just evolved from a million years into the banana that it is? Food for you? Just perfect fuel for you to digest, that just so happens to have all the nutrients that you need.

Okay, have you had enough thinking about the things down here? How about looking up at the stars like never before? Notice how magnificent they are. How amazing they are. Scientists are saying now that they are not random, but that they actually have a complex order. How brilliant. Scientists are finding out more and more about them every day. Just think about how man said, "I want to go up there and land on the moon." How crazy! Who even had time to think of how to do that? I mean, seriously, that was before all the modern conveniences and easy access to information. I mean, come on now, I am having trouble finding time to look at a tree!

Think about how a plane flies in the air and stays up in the sky with people sitting on it. Pick up a pencil, and I can tell you that it falls quickly to the floor. I know some of you think about that all too well when you are in the plane, hoping to God, you will make it to your destination! Or think of a how a boat can hold people and not sink, yet a small crack can cause such devastation. Yes, you people of science, I know there are laws of science and far more things than my mind can imagine or comprehend, but let's just stay with the amazement of it for a little while. The design of it. It is so amazing that there are laws of science to allow us to figure all this out. That there are math calculations and formulas and all that crazy stuff to make it possible. What is math? God, I hate math. I have a doctorate degree, but I most likely have the math ability of a fourth grader. But I appreciate it. I appreciate math because of the complex, yet perfect system of it. It was created for us to be able to explore, create, and design things. Think of all the laws of science. Just think of all we have learned over the last several hundred years and all the great inventions we now have. Think of all the great scientists, such as Newton and Einstein, some of them who lived just in the past hundred years or so. Think of how far technology has come. How much more is out there that we don't know? What things have we not yet discovered? What things do we think we know, but we actually don't? Who created the laws that science is subject to? The questions go on and on. Think of colors. What are they? Okay, I will stop. I am hoping I gave you enough to contemplate today!

So, get to work. Remember, you are dying in eight days. What do you really want to look at and notice? What do you really want to see? Your family? Your children? *Really* look at them. Dig in and journal. What do you notice? Be a child, like you are looking at everything for the first time! Really open your eyes and see. See with your mind, not your eyes. Go!

Wait, slow down! I got ahead of myself. While we are talking about noticing things, I think it's important to discuss the concept of perception. What is perception? According to the dictionary, perception is the ability to see, hear, or become aware of something through the senses, or it is the state of being or the process of becoming aware of something through the senses. Think of the jungle scenario. You might have felt lost from your vantage point, but if you'd had the bigger picture, the vantage point of a map, or even a helicopter, the view would be very different. You would have seen things from a different perspective. For example, let's think of earth. We used to think it was flat, until we found another perspective. From outer space, we can see that it's round. Perception is not always what it appears to be. I mean, we could be dangling upside right now on the earth, but we don't see it. An interesting fact here is that the Bible, which was written two thousand years ago, mentioned the earth being round, even before we discovered that was true. My point is that science see things only from the perspective it has at the time. If someone would have told a scientist two thousand years ago that there would be a microwave that heats up food in two minutes, they wouldn't have believed it. They only knew what they knew at the time. Immaculate conception seemed like an outrageous concept, but I can tell you with 100 percent certainty it can be done. I know for sure at least one person who has had a child without being with a man, through the modern miracle of artificial insemination. We often laugh at things we don't understand. We tell people they are foolish for believing things they cannot see or understand. But again, it's just that "we don't know what we don't know." Science is only as good as what we know at that point in time, from our perspective. It is arrogant to think you know everything or that science is 100 percent fact. Much of it is just theory.

Could it be foolish to believe that everything could be so perfectly designed? Or foolish to think the earth and everything in it just randomly fell into place with a great big bang? Or just evolved over millions of years to be so perfect? As I once read somewhere, that would be similar to throwing a bunch of parts in the air, and believing they just randomly aligned with each other to create an object like a bike or a car. Even if there are a bunch of random moving parts, you would need a creator to put it together correctly, right? Okay, enough for now. Go! Run! Have fun! But don't trip. Keep your perspective.

IF ONLY?

Self-Reflection Questions

1. Assess your surroundings. What is something you noticed today that you never noticed before?

2. Do you really think, after looking at everything around you, that all of this just randomly arrived out of a "big bang," or that it slowly evolved into what it is today, or is there a possibility that there is a Creator behind it all?

3. If there is a Creator, do you feel that you worship the Creator or the creation in your life?

4. When you meditate, do you focus inside yourself, or do you take the time to meditate on the beauty that is around you?

5. If you truly only had eight more days to live, is there something you would like to take notice of in more detail?

6. What stops you from taking the time to notice these things, and what can you do to change it?

7. What is something that stood out for you in the reading today?

8. What are some more questions you have?

9. How can you learn more about it?

10. Now for the "if only" question: What would you have done differently today if you had known you'd be gone in eight days?

CHAPTER 4

Who Are You Really?

My stepfather, who raised me, was a patient man. He was the kind of man who, if you wanted a special kind of coffee, he would drive to the next state to get it for you. He was the most patient man I ever knew—until 1998. That year he was in a head-on collision and was never the same. He was not very different, but he was different enough. He was slightly less patient. His eyes looked different, too—a little bigger. He didn't understand the world as much anymore. He said it was different.

After that happened to him, I became fascinated with the way the mind works, and I completed the school neuropsychology track in my doctorate program. We are just now beginning to understand all the complexities of our brains. Now, in the 2000s, with advances in neuroscience, we are starting to understand just how truly amazing the brain really is. In the 1800s, we still thought the human heart was the center of the body, the center of our thoughts and feelings. Now we understand that the brain is much more. We understand how each part is so delicately put together, how each area is responsible for certain functions, such as vision, speech, hearing, or understanding speech. If a neurosurgeon is performing surgery on your brain and makes one wrong move, you might never speak again. Think of how precise that is! Think how intricately your brain is wired. It is like the best computer ever made. But with one fall, one slip, one small bleed in the brain, we become different people. A few sips of alcohol or drugs can alter your mind and perception too.

Your task today is to think of the human brain for more than two minutes. Spend some time on this. Think of how your brain is such a complex system of neural circuitry. Think of how your brain literally has wires (or nerves) connecting it to other parts of your body. If you tell your arm and hand to pick up a glass of water, they pick it up. If you see something scary, it automatically sends your body into a state of fight or flight. You literally turn into the Incredible Hulk. You didn't think that could really happen, did you? But yes, you turn into the Hulk. Your eyes dilate to have better vision, your blood flows to your muscles to make them react faster, and your digestion stops. You may even become nauseous. You breathe heavier. You are ready for either flight or fight. I have seen and worked with

IF ONLY?

many adults and children who struggle with this crazy sensation. They report they are just standing around at work, at school, or in the community, and for no reason at all, they suddenly turn into the Hulk. They may try to escape these feelings by staying home or running to the nurse at school. Some may even visit the emergency room. These sensations are so uncomfortable and so anxiety-producing that many people even seek out therapy—all in attempt to avoid this crazy process that our autonomic nervous system kicks off. But how amazing it is to think that your nervous system takes in all the information in the world around you. And then it sends a message to your muscles to protect you!

Our bodies are amazing. Just think of the ability of our brains to hold information. What is that? What is a memory? It is literally just a bunch of electrical activity in one part of our brain. And some people think we just arrived here out of nothing? Okay, let's open our minds a bit. Do you really think our brains, as complex as they are, just randomly designed themselves? An assorted mass of cells started with electrical activity and became something out of nothing? Human beings can build amazing computers with the capacity to hold nearly an infinite amount of information, but we also know those computers are created and designed. They didn't just appear out of nothing. That would be crazy! If a brand-new computer landed on your desk tomorrow, you would know that someone put it there. Some may find me naïve to suggest that someone put us here on earth, but I think it is naïve to think someone didn't. It just doesn't make any sense. Our minds are electrical and chemical. Think of that for a second. Our brains are made up of cells that send electrical messages to each other through neurons. Your brain has almost a hundred billion neurons! According to one source, a neuron fires about two hundred times per second, and each neuron connects to about one thousand other neurons. Think of how many bits of information that is transmitted per second! The electrical activity can also be measured by very sensitive recoding tools called electrodes, which measure brainwaves using an EEG. Specific frequencies can determine certain clinical disorders in certain areas of the brain, including seizures, anxiety, ADHD, etc. We literally were designed like computers (or computers were designed after us). Something or someone designed us for greatness, designed us for a purpose. What is interesting is that we get infected, like computers do. We get viruses. Anyone who has struggled with a mental health affliction such as anxiety, a panic disorder, or clinical depression, especially with psychosis, will for sure tell you it's the truth. They often complain they can't think right. In fact, ECT is still the gold standard for treating depression with psychosis. And no, it is not just a bunch of electricity surged into your brain. The goal is to produce a seizure, which literally reboots your brain. Your brain literally, in some circumstances, needs to be shut off temporarily and then turned back on again. Doctors are unsure why this is so effective, but sometimes it is the only thing that works. Now, I am not simply suggesting we are walking robots. My point is that we are amazing creatures. We were created, for sure.

I recently bought a neurofeedback machine for my practice. In minutes, your scalp is hooked up to an EEG with nineteen channels of electrodes placed on your head that measure your brain waves. The machine then compares your brain to the normative sample of others. It tells you what parts of your brain are efficient and what are not, then it unconsciously trains your brain waves to work more efficiently. How cool is that? Please just think of that for fifteen minutes today. What does that mean?

Electricity is a part of our everyday existence. It produces power and lights in our homes and businesses. What is light? It is a type of electromagnetic wave that can carry energy from one place to another and can be perceived by the human eye. Think about that for a second, and what things cannot be perceived?

Ponder on the ability to pick up your cell phone and call a relative in a different state or even a different country and connect with them in seconds! In just seconds, their voice can be instantly heard. I know there is a scientific explanation. But just think of that as a process. In seconds, you can talk to anyone in the world. All you have to do is pick up the phone. If you don't pick up the phone, you won't get a signal and you will not hear anything. You cannot see how the electricity gets there, but that doesn't mean it is not real. I can't see how a memory is made, but it's still there. It's electrical. How does a camera make a picture? It works by capturing that light through a lens and projecting it and recording it, or, in the case of television, translating it into electrical impulses. It saves that one moment in time and captures it forever. Our minds do that too. But how? It's part electrical.

So, what does this mean? What am I telling you? I don't know exactly what I am trying to say, other than just think about who you are. Think about the successes of electrical activity that defines you. Think of how your brain has captured bad memories, maybe even trauma, everything you have been through. Just think of how what happened to you ten or twenty years ago is a mass of electrical activity that still impacts you today! But the brain is capable of change and growth. It is amazing. You were born a blank slate, to be filled with lots of things. But you don't know what you are capable of. You are capable of amazing things, because you were created. So now, think about your life. Think about you—

your body, your brain. You only have seven more days to live! Don't only think of your brain, but think of your body, too. How wonderfully awesome it was created, to eat for fuel, to get rid of the by-products, and to maintain all the processes needed to keep you alive!

By the way, I didn't even touch upon my nana. She is 102 years old and counting, and she still lives alone! I am reminded of my clothing dryer that I really wanted. It was so shiny and red, and it seemed like a great machine at the time that I bought it. It lasted four years. FOUR years. Think of all your household appliances. How long do they last? Ten to twenty years at best? My nana... Her body has lasted 102 years and counting! I mean, what a wonderful Creator we have, who could make a human heart that beats for one hundred years—unstoppable—along with all the other organs that make up the human body. I would like to know who was on quality-control check the day Nana was born!

Here are some more fascinating things to think about. We are learning more and more about the brain and body every day. Real understanding of the brain has just begun with all the technology that we have in today's world. We are also learning more about DNA and our unique genetic code. However, there is still so much more to learn. If we knew everything about our bodies, we could cure all diseases. What amazing things will we do in the future that we don't even know about yet?

What are dreams? Why do we all go to bed at night and literally recharge? Like aliens in a space pod, we lie down in our beds and go off to another time and place, filled with electrical activity. Dreams are still one of the great complexities and questions of mankind. If we are electrical, can we download other things, other sources of electricity? What do I mean by that? If there is a God, would it be possible that He could download some sort of power into us? Change our thinking? Change what has "input" into us? It is interesting to consider that the Bible tells us we are new creatures, literally a new creation, if we are "in Christ" (see 2 Corinthians 5:17). That is just something to think about and consider.

Again, I want to say that science is amazing. We all want to search for these answers and understand these things. But science is only as good as the human who searches for it, as well as the capacity of our understanding at the time. Some things we just have to trust rather than fully understand. We don't know what we don't know yet. We have to trust the others before us who knew the secrets. But who actually knows the secrets of the universe? We will get to that tomorrow. But for now, ponder—about yourself! You only have seven days left! I challenge you to just take a few minutes and ponder these simple facts. Your challenge today is to sit down for fifteen minutes and think about you and the amazing creation that you are. You were designed for amazing things. Like trees, people come in all types, and not all are created alike or have the same purpose. What is *your* computer-like brain like? What are your strengths? What are your weaknesses? We will get to your purpose soon enough.

Self-Reflection Questions

1. Who are you? What is your personality like? What are you good at? What can you do well?

2. What are your weaknesses, and areas of need for growth?

3. What experiences have shaped you, both positively and negatively?

4. Do you think there is a way you can reshape your brain and neural circuitry?

5. Do you think after considering all the complexities of the human mind and body that there is the possibility a Creator exists?

6. For what purpose do you think you might have been created?

IF ONLY?

7. What is something that stood out in the reading?

8. What are some more questions you have?

9. How can you learn more about it?

10. Now for the "if only" question: What would you have done differently today if you had known you'd be gone in seven days?

CHAPTER 5

Where Did I Come From?

I was about three or four years old. This may sound weird, but I remember sitting on the kitchen floor. My parents were sitting at the kitchen table. I was just sitting there, thinking, "I am here." I had just realized that I was *actually there*. Now, I don't think I was even able to understand where "here" meant, but I still remember having that sensation at such a young age—the feeling that I was there. I am not sure how I got there, but I had the keen awareness that I was somewhere different.

I often think back on that memory and wonder, "Where is here, and how did I get here?" Have you ever wondered that? How you physically, mentally, spiritually got to this place? And of course, I am not talking about the birds and the bees. I mean beyond that. Our souls. The outer layer and physical body are easy. Anyone can do that. We can even create people in wax museums. We can create artificial arms and legs. But I am talking about the very essence of our being. I am talking about the electricity and neural circuitry of who we are. There are some people today who believe that in the not-so-distant future, we will be able to artificially create the human brain, or robots that can imitate the human brain, using nanotechnology. Funny how we can understand that, but yet we shrug at the thought of a Creator. We judge people who believe in a Creator as people who believe in fairy tales. But we didn't know what we didn't know a thousand years ago and look how far we have come in technology today. Is it so hard to believe in a Creator now that we know what we know now? Is it so hard to believe that someone or something outside of us created us in His image?

Here is some more food for thought. Think about your past. Where is "here"? Think back on your earliest memories. Funny how they are just pieces of electrical activity in your brains. Our memories are just tiny tidbits of electric activity stored in a small part of our brain called the hippocampus. However, for many of us, those memories haunt us forever. Those few short seconds in time can have such a lasting effect. For some of us, they carry the emotions of guilt, shame, sadness, trauma, fear, and anger. Other memories are filled with thoughts of sweetness, happiness, love, and appreciation. How funny it is that simple electrical impulses—memories—can impact our daily function. But how?

How did we get to where we are now? Physically, mentally, and spiritually.

Physically, we understand that we have a body that grows wonderfully and strong. I have two teenage daughters, and just to look at them brings me to such wonder. I look at their healthy, beautiful, tall, slender bodies, with skin as smooth as silk, and I find myself questioning the answer I already know. Was I really ever that beautiful? Did I ever look that young? Was my skin ever that smooth? Was I ever that skinny? I look in the mirror now and know that I am just destined to die. My skin is sagging, and there are wrinkles across my face and body. I try to pull them back, but I know that's only temporary. I look at my worn-out body, almost a hundred pounds heavier than I once was. A hundred pounds! How did I get to this place? It didn't take long. Every morsel in my mouth went right to my hips. That's how I got to this place! Man, why didn't I enjoy my skinny body when I had it. I thought I was fat, even back then. Don't we all? I get out of bed now, and my ankles hurt. My bones hurt. To get to the bathroom in the morning is a chore. I know part of that is the weight, but I know I am not the only one who suffers. It happens to all of us—because we are destined to grow old. It's inevitable. Our bodies are only temporary. When you are young, it's so hard to imagine. If only I had enjoyed it back then. *If only*. There are those words again. If only

I had known how beautiful I was. How young I looked, how good my bones felt. But I didn't know what to compare it to back then. I didn't know what I didn't know. I only had the time I was in to compare it to. If only I would have enjoyed it. Really savored it. I tell my girls all the time. Enjoy it. Take it in. Relish how strong you feel and how fast you are. How beautifully made you are. But we are just shells. Just bodies, destined to die. Like trees. We are like wonderful blossoms of youth, filled with magnificent flowers of pink and gold and beautiful fruit. Summer comes upon us, and we are in full bloom, hearty and green and full of life. Some of us are beaten down by the hot sun. Torched by the heat or flooded by the rain, but we endure. However, fall comes, and with it there is the luminous fact that it's getting cold outside and winter will soon be upon us. Winter is coming. The leaves, although so beautiful in their splendor, are just the sure sign and physical reminder that there is only a limited time left. One by one, the leaves (each of us) start falling away. Slowly at first, but then as the great wind comes, it whisks more of us away. Day by day, winter comes closer, and we know that soon it will all be gone. Winter is such a beautiful time, but it is also so cold, ugly, and silent. We tuck ourselves inside our houses and try not to think about it. But we know it's coming. Just as winter comes, so does that fact that we know we are mortal. Our lives will end, and our bodies will fail. Our bones will shatter; we will decay. That is a fact. Physically, that is a fact. In what season are you in your life? I know I am just ending summer. Fall has its beauty, but I know my days are numbered.

Physically, I know how I got here in this place in my life and how I arrived (birds and bees). But I am talking about something more. I love the poem about two twin babies who, while in the womb, had a conversation about what would be waiting on the other side when they were born. One of them questions that there is anything on the other side. The other one is sure there is something. And they argue. In the womb we live in a pool of water, sucking the lifeline of our mothers' umbilical cord. Just waiting. Waiting for who knows what? But then there is birth. And the life cycle starts. We are destined to die. But what about all that electricity? How did that get here? How about our soul? How about our emotions? When did that start? Where does that go?

I remember a high school psychology teacher who used to ask the following question. If energy can neither be created nor destroyed, where does it go? It simply changes states. So, remember, we have a physical existence, but can we also have an emotional and spiritual existence? Could that be those electrical impulses? Where do they come from? Where do they go? What are they? So many questions. Just some fascinating questions to think about.

IF ONLY?

I know we thought briefly about how you physically got here. But let's talk about your emotional and spiritual life. Where are you? Have you had a hard life mentally? What has shaped you personally at your core being? Have you had bad experiences? Have you had a good life or a bad life? Do you question how you got to this place?

I am a shy person. Anyone would say so. I dare you to go to anyone from the Hamburg area high school and ask about Leslie Schlegel. The first thing they will probably say is "Who?" No one even knew me. I was too shy. Now, ask about my brother or mother, and they will surely say yes. My mother was a hairdresser in the town, and my brother was, well, just Brett: outgoing, funny, the life of the party. But not me. I was awkward, overweight, with buck teeth and braces. I didn't ever know what to say. I was a late bloomer. I thrived in college, more so probably because nobody knew the old me. But how could I go from the old me to the me I am now? I told you before, I wanted to be a counselor, so my life took on a life of its own with school, more school, kids, and more school. I finally got to the place where I wanted to open a private practice, and I did. Actually, I opened two group practices and I am a leader of almost twenty clinicians. That was not my original plan, but I ended up here. How did that happen?

Several years ago, I applied to a local university to teach. Why I even applied, I am not sure. Something must have appealed to me subconsciously—or maybe I was led there—so I applied. To my dismay, two weeks before the semester started, they called me in for an interview. I had plans to go to the zoo the next day with my kids. I cried. I didn't want to go to the interview. Why had I even applied for the job? "I can't teach," I thought to myself. "I am shy. My brother even said I wouldn't be good at it. Why, again, did I apply for this job?"

I argued with my husband, who told me to go to the interview and just see what it was about. He said it didn't mean I had to take the job. I went, not at all happy that I was missing the zoo. But I went anyway. I didn't like the basement of the university. I wasn't taking the job, I told myself sternly. I knew that much as I sat on the chair waiting for the faculty to come take me away. Ugh! Why had I wasted my day on this? You see, it wasn't just an interview; it was a daylong affair. Not only did I have three separate meetings with different faculty members, I had to provide a sample of my teaching in front of everyone. I had never taught a day in my life. You can see why I cried. I fought that one. But there I was. Nope. This job was not for me, I kept arguing with myself.

It was the end of the day, and I was sitting for my last interview. The professor who had originally called me to set up the interview was sitting beside me. In an attempt to make small talk to avoid the awkward silence, he said, "Thanks for calling." What? What was he talking about?

I hadn't called him. He appeared to think I'd called to check on the status of my application. I can assure you; that wasn't me. Never. With that, I was whisked away to my last interview, where they discussed the salary. While professors are never rich, what they offered was surely more than I had been making before. Before I knew it, I was a college professor. And it turned out to be one of the best jobs I ever had. Exposure therapy at its finest. Who knew?

How did I get there? Life circumstances for sure, coupled with some successive learning experiences in my brain. In addition to some random acts of fate and taking chances. Or was it divine intervention?

My mind has grown over the years. I have learned things through my experiences. I have lived, I have laughed, I have cried. I have grown physically (an understatement), mentally, and spiritually. You heard my spiritual story earlier. But what about you? How did you get here? Physically, mentally, spiritually? What life experiences have shaped you in how you got to this place? We will talk later about why you are here. But the question for today is, How did you get here? Look back and really think about that question. Your task for today is to make a timeline of how you got to the place you are at right now. What memories or life events shaped and molded you into who, what, and where you are at right now? Spend time reflecting on that. What have you learned? Remember, if I had known that was the last time I would have seen my father, I would have held him a little longer. Or I would have appreciated those last few moments together. If you look back on how you got here, would you have done something different? Would you have appreciated the time, or would you have wished you didn't go through that experience? But remember, it has shaped you! You are you because of it, good or bad, right or wrong. Often, it's more about what you do with the experiences, how they have shaped you, and what lessons you have learned from it. Maybe it was supposed to happen in order to lead you to this very place?

Our pastor preached a sermon many years ago that resonated with me. He spoke of a painter creating a big picture. The painter used a lot of black. Someone standing behind the painter made a statement that it was an ugly picture and dark. The person behind the painter was being judgmental. They were being critical of the picture because it wasn't colorful or pretty enough. It just wasn't good. He waited longer, and as the picture unfolded, a great portrait of a beautiful sunset appeared. The creator needed that ugly black color to accent the beauty of the picture. What would a beautiful sunset be if it didn't contrast with the different colors? The creator needed that. He needed those ugly colors. He knew what he was doing because he alone was the creator.

IF ONLY?

If we are created, we are created for a purpose. We are not just random pieces of nothing, but we were created and are being woven together like a quilt to be perfect. Maybe we have not had the experiences we wanted, but we are not the creators; we are merely the colors in the pictures. We don't know what our pictures will look like at the end. But if we are created, we must trust the process. We must believe that Someone greater than us knows better. We know the picture will be great when it's done. We are all masterpieces in the works.

How does all of this answer the question of where we came from? I do not have that answer, but I do know the picture is not completed yet. We can only look at where you have come from in this life and to see what you have learned from it so far. That is how you can know where you have come from. I can tell you that there are just too many things about the universe that we don't understand. Some sources say that we only understand 5 percent of the universe. We could have come from anywhere, but maybe the bigger question is not, where did we come from, but why are we here.

We will get to that question soon. But for today, I want you to meditate on the question, Where did I come from, and how did I get here? Remember you only have six days to live now!

Self-Reflection Questions

1. Where are you now in your life—physically, emotionally, and spiritually—and where did you come from? Make a timeline of the life experiences that have shaped you (both good and bad).

2. What is one experience that stands out as having had the most impact on your life?

3. What did you learn from that life experience?

4. If you could take one life experience away from what you have lived through, what would it be and why?

5. How would you be different if you didn't have that life experience?

6. How do you think you could use that negative experience to impact others in a positive way?

7. What is something that stood out in the reading?

8. What are some more questions you have?

9. How can you learn more about it?

10. Now for the "if only" question: What would you have done differently today if you had known you'd be gone in six days?

CHAPTER 6

Why Am I Here?

I don't remember exactly what day or year it was, but I remember waking up thinking I wanted to be a psychologist. I didn't remember any dream. I just knew I woke up with that feeling. Of course, I had the experience of the social worker who had made me say goodbye to my dad. But I really hadn't thought too much of her at the time. This day, combined with that experience, defined my future existence. Why? I don't know exactly, but I am here at this place in my life today.

I often think of my life and how it would be different if my father hadn't died when he did. Would I be still a psychologist? Would I be at this place physically, emotionally, and spiritually? What would my life be like if that had not happened at all? That part of my life shaped me. It shaped my future. I might not have liked it. But I am here today because of that experience—and the same is true of you and your experiences. Without all of them, good and bad, you would be a different person. Yes, perhaps you would have the same personality traits, but for sure you would be different. I can't answer the questions of why you are here or where you are headed on this earth, but I do know you have been given a purpose.

There are some people who study time. These researchers found that some people spend most of their time focusing on the past. They live in the past. They lament about the past. They have trouble getting over the past. They are stuck. They often live with feelings of regret, anger, and all sorts of negative emotions the past has caused. Then there are some people who live in the present. They don't consider the future consequences of their actions. They live only for today, like tomorrow will never come. Then still others focus more on the future. While this can be positive in some ways, they often forget to enjoy the present. Which type of person are you?

Let's focus a bit on the people who live in the past. Some people spend way too much time here, thinking of all the heartache they have been through. It's easy to get stuck in the past. However, that can prevent you from seeing any purpose for the future.

Maybe for you, though, it's not all about the past. Maybe it's more about the present and the future. Maybe it's more about what you do with your past life experiences that matters the most. Maybe that is the purpose for what you have been through in your life.

WHY AM I HERE?

Think of how long fruit lasts? Days, maybe? But it still serves a purpose. A sunflower can last only a few months, but its beauty is inspiring. The sunset is gone in moments, but the memories of it can last a lifetime. We all have a purpose. We were all created for something. Just because you don't know your purpose yet doesn't mean you don't have one. It just means you haven't searched hard enough for it. Also remember—maybe it's not all about you. Maybe your purpose is for someone else, to be at the right time and place for another who might need you.

Did you ever think about the purpose of the cycle of life? We all love to hear the news of someone who is having a baby and how excited they are. They are full of anticipation, full of fear, full of wonder. After the baby is born, watching the child grow is an incredible journey, especially if you are a parent. The joy your children can give you is unmeasurable. I'm not saying that it's not filled with disappointment too. Children can crush your heart like no one else. As a mom, I have cried many tears over my kids. Most parents would give their children anything, even die for them, and still, kids can be so mean, so hurtful, so selfish. Yet, we still love them with our whole hearts. When they go off to college, we watch them go with lumps in our throats. They are going to learn to become young men and woman; they are going to change, mature, and grow. They will do things that we may not agree with, but they have to learn those things for themselves. We have to let them go, let them spread their wings and fly. They will go on to have children and grandchildren themselves. They will have careers, friends, and family, and then they, too, will grow old. Again, some of us know this feeling all too well. But what is our purpose in this life—just to live and then die?

Think of all that you have become over the years in your life. Think of all the wisdom you have acquired throughout your lifetime. Some of us never learn. But maybe that is what our brains are designed for: to learn and to grow. We have a blank slate when we are born, meant to be filled with the things that we learn. Every day we make more connections, we make more memories. The electrical activity in our bodies is getting stronger and stronger, and even more connections are made. If we think of it like that, maybe that is our purpose. Maybe our purpose is *to learn*. Learning is the process of acquiring new knowledge, understanding, behaviors, skills, values, attitudes, and preferences, through experience or study. But what are we supposed to learn? Maybe we go through certain experiences to learn something for ourselves. But maybe it's even more important to have these experiences in order to help others. My father's death, though it was so very painful for me, helped countless others.

WHY AM I HERE?

I am inspired by the Adam Walsh story. Adam was a little boy who was abducted in a grocery store and later found murdered. What purpose could that have possibly served? Adam's father, John Walsh, went on to become an amazing advocate for victims of violent crime and the host of *America's Most Wanted*, a television show that aided in the capture of thousands of fugitives. John Walsh has helped countless numbers of victimized children because of what happened to his son. I am not sure why his son was killed in such an inhumane way, but John was able to use that learning experience and what happened to him to help others. That is *purpose*.

What learning experiences have you had that shaped who you are? What learning experiences have you had that can make you helpful to others? The best teachers are those who have had the same experiences. I taught college for a short time, and my students liked me because I could give them real experiences as examples of what they were learning. It was more helpful information to them than the ideas discussed in textbooks about theory. I could share with them real, heartfelt stories and experiences that had happened to me in the field. Perhaps you are learning now in order to be a teacher to others someday. Again, what have you learned, and how can you help others?

Maybe that is why it is worth it to grow old, gray, feeble, and weak. Older people sure do have a lot of wisdom. If only we would take the time to listen and heed their advice. This is your chance. Remember you only have five days left. Learn from others who have gone through difficult experiences. What was their purpose? Maybe they can help you!

The other day, one of my daughters made the comment that if she were to become a quadriplegic, she would rather just die. I reminded her about Nick Vujicic, a man born with a rare disorder that resulted in the absence of his arms and legs. What was the purpose of that disorder in his life? Well, I can tell you he will be remembered far longer than most of us, and it had nothing to do with his arms or legs. His life was an amazing testament to his character and purpose in life. And he now helps others to find the purpose in their lives. Now, that is getting purpose out of nothing! Purpose can be found, but you do have to look for it. Some of you may ask, Why is my child intellectually disabled? What is the purpose of that? Only you can find purpose in that experience. But again, maybe the purpose isn't for *your child*. Maybe the purpose is for you, to learn patience, love, dedication, and humor.

I will end with one more personal story for those of you who may be struggling. Many years ago, my husband had a depressive episode with psychosis. I remember the night when it all came to a head. He had been struggling with some medical issues that had not been

WHY AM I HERE?

resolved, and he awoke from sleep one night thinking that Satan was literally coming for him. He ran out of the house with no shoes, and then sprinted toward the Appalachian Mountain range, behind our house. I sank to my knees. I had never fainted before, but this was the first time I almost did. My mind was spinning, trying to comprehend that this was really happening. This was my life? It had to be somebody else's. But it was true.

I will never forget the solemn faces of the police officers. "He's as normal as you," I said. "He's as normal as you." I couldn't believe what had just happened. My mom took my arm and walked me inside the house, and I crawled upstairs to the toilet, sick to my stomach. I was going to throw up. I mean me—the one who can eat through stress—yet there I was, hunched over the toilet. I took a breath. Nothing came out. I sat down beside the toilet and just waited. They were looking for him, who was lost on a mountain in shorts and bare feet. Where was he? How would they even look for him? It was about two o'clock in the morning. They would have had the helicopters out in the search, but it was too windy. There was just a group of police officers searching the mountain in the dark.

Thankfully, they did find him a few hours later. My husband, whom we used to laugh about and say he was the most normal out of the bunch of us, was whisked away and kept in the hospital for several weeks. Just writing about this time in our lives gives me the chills. I remember screaming at God every night: "Why, why, why?" I had always prepared myself in my mind for death. My husband or I were going to die early. I knew it—that was just a fact. I had learned that with my life experience. People died young of cancer. I had found purpose in that. I could see that clearly and the purpose made sense. It shaped me. Simple. My death or that of my husband would one day shape my children. That made perfect sense to me.

But what was the purpose of this experience I was going through now? I was pretty good at finding purpose in a lot of things. But what was the purpose of this? It didn't make any sense. Divorce? I had never thought of it before, but I thought about it then. Who was this man I was married to? A robot lately, it seemed. He wasn't the person he used to be. He had lost fifty pounds, and he could neither sleep, nor eat. They checked him for a tumor. Yes, see—I knew he was going to die. I think on some level, I wanted it to be a tumor. Then at least it would make more sense. The experience would have had purpose. But this just didn't make any sense.

I knew God didn't like divorce. So why would He put us through this? Because, more than ever, was I thinking about divorce. I was lonely without my husband. This man wasn't the husband that I knew. Why would he do such a thing? We had never had any problems before besides maybe a financial argument here and there, but I had seriously sometimes thought he was an angel sent by God. We were perfect for each other. Two peas in a pod. So, why this?

His whole personality changed. He focused on his health day and night, and there was nothing I could say or do to help. We would go out to eat, and he would just sit there and stare. I felt so alone. I know he was struggling with his own internal afflictions, but I was struggling, too. I can't explain how lonely I felt. I was angry at God, that He would cause me to have such awful, selfish feelings, and I just couldn't understand it, not for the life of me.

Our pastor came over one night after my husband returned home from the hospital, only to return back again. After a short remission, his symptoms had come back with a vengeance. The pastor said, "Perhaps there is more learning to be done." Well, heck, I thought, I had already learned a lot. I still didn't see any point in it at all. The whole thing had disrupted our life. I knew enough about depression. I was a social worker and a psychologist, for God's sake. I didn't need to be taught anything more. I knew everything there was to know about depression and anxiety—or so I thought. Boy, was I wrong!

I still thank God every day for that experience. Not that I would ever want to go through it again—but I wouldn't trade it! I have found, as a psychologist, I am 100 percent better from having gone through that season with my husband. I am more empathetic. I now truly understand how crippling anxiety and depression can be to people and their family members. I had just spent $250,000 on a doctorate degree, but no amount of money or knowledge could have fully prepared me for that experience. It helped me to truly understand the devastation people go through, the pure hell they experience. My husband is 100 percent fine now. We have a happy and fulfilled marriage, but boy, did I question everything at the time.

My point is that maybe the purpose is all about the learning—expanding our brains, expanding our knowledge with experiences. Without learning, life would be pretty boring. Isn't it the dips that make the roller coasters fun in the end? Going up that long descent, only to plunge to the depths for a few seconds—but it makes it fun! Learning is hard work; it isn't all fun and games. It can be downright scary. What sticks to us is usually what we get wrong, not what we get right. What sticks is the hard times, not all the fun and games.

Researchers say that people who find meaning in their lives have more positive outcomes. Even Viktor Frankl, a Holocaust victim, in his book *Man's Search for Meaning*, asserted that the primary psychological motivation for life is the search for meaning. He believed that finding meaning in suffering was powerful. He also believed that suffering ceases the moment it finds meaning; it is not our situations that determine our future, but our attitude toward the challenges we face. Each of us has a choice in how to react.

I would like to add one last story as food for thought. If we (with our amazing brains, built for so much potential) were left here on this amazing planet called Earth, and we are expected to learn and grow, in order to fulfill some sort of purpose, we wouldn't want to forget our Creator, if there was one, right?

I think it would be similar to having children and years later, sending them off to college. We drop them off with tears in our eyes. The tears flow because we know it is their time to find themselves. It's their time to fly. But it's also scary because we, as parents, lose that sense of control. Our children have to do things for themselves now. What if they fail? What if they succeed? Or, worst of all, what if they don't need us anymore? What if they don't ever call or come home again? What if we lose them forever?

Inevitably, things will change because they are off to learn new things. They are going to have wonderful life-changing experiences, or so we hope. But how sad it would be if they never thought of us?

I challenge you to consider this question. What if someone created us for a purpose, whether it is learning or something else. How sad it would be if we never thought of them. How sad they would be if we forgot about them. How sad it would be if the Creator thought we didn't need Him anymore. If we never looked back to where we came from. If only some of us would reach out to the Creator and check in with Him. Ask for His help. Ask for His assistance. Ask Him to reveal your purpose to you. What were you made for?

My oldest daughter had just started college when all the fear about COVID-19 ramped up, and her classes were all moved to online, distance learning. She ultimately decided to live at home for her first semester. As she logged on for her first orientation class, she couldn't get the sound to work on her Zoom account. *Ha!* I thought. *She needs me! She needs me!* How good it felt for that short moment that she had asked for my help. Now, it was just that moment of time, and then, of course, it was gone and she was back to her independent self. But she had needed me!

Don't we all like to be needed in some way? As her mother, I would never steer my daughter in the wrong direction. I want to help her. I am just waiting and hoping she will ask me for directions or for guidance if she ever needs it. Maybe *you* should check in "at home" with the One who created you. Ask for directions if you are lost... Make the call... You only have five days left to check in. Ask away. Take the time to reconnect with Him.

Self-Reflection Questions

1. In terms of time, do you live too much in the past, do you only consider the present, or do you focus exclusively on the future?

2. What is your purpose?

3. How can you use your experiences—good and bad—to help others?

4. Would helping others give you more meaning and purpose? Why?

5. What have you learned from others with more experience than you?

6. If there is a Creator, do you think you should check in with Him? Why or why not?

7. What is something that stood out in the reading?

8. What are some more questions you have?

9. How can you learn more about it?

10. Now for the "if only" question: What would you have done differently today if you had known you'd be gone in five days?

CHAPTER 7

Where Am I Going?

It was the summer of 2012. The car was jam-packed. We had three weeks—three weeks for the journey of a lifetime. I had packed at least three weeks' worth of underwear. I made sure we had enough snacks for the long drive, sweatshirts in case it was cold, and of course, coloring books and maps and games for the girls. It was going to be a long ride. I had planned, and planned, and planned. I remember sitting by my mom's pool for hours, plotting out the course. There were so many ways to go. How would we get there? Which way was the fastest? Which way would have the least amount of traffic? Which one was the most direct route?

I walked into AAA at the time, my "great agenda" all laid out. I actually went to two separate AAA offices with the long list of places I wanted to go. One of the travel agents at one of the offices told me it was impossible, that we wouldn't get it all done in three weeks' time. I went to another office while I was working one day in a different area. This other travel agent was excited. She had never attempted to help anyone with such high expectations to visit so many places in one vacation. But she *did* help me. I think I was in her office about two hours that day, as we planned everything out very carefully. It was so exciting! I knew where we were going—on a great Western vacation, and while we were there, we were going see everything that we possibly could!

It did turn out to be a once-in-a-lifetime trip—the best trip ever. It was flawless. Not once in three weeks did we get stuck in traffic or get lost. I still can't believe it. But that was because I had it all mapped out. I spent weeks carefully planning out every detail. I spent countless hours stretched over AAA maps, charting our course and following the agent's suggestions. We started in Pennsylvania and stopped in Tennessee at Dollywood. Then it was on to Texas so I could take a test for my diplomate in school neuropsychology. We then traveled to New Mexico, visited the Grand Canyon in Arizona, and then we were off to Utah to see the beautiful Bryce Canyon, Zion National Park, and up past the Grand Tetons to Wyoming and Montana to visit Yellowstone National Park. We then traveled over to South Dakota to see Mount Rushmore and then down to Colorado to visit my family. Finally, we headed home on the last, long stretch across the country back to Pennsylvania. Three weeks and eight thousand miles later, we were home.

It was a great vacation. But here's the kicker: It wouldn't have worked out nearly as well if I hadn't known exactly where we were going every day. I had meticulously charted out each day's itinerary, right down to exactly where we were going to eat and spend the night. And that was half the fun—the planning! It filled us with anticipation and hope. I can honestly say that for that three-week vacation, I spent at least a month planning it out.

Now, I cannot tell you for sure exactly where you are going after this life. Some of you may think we are going nowhere except straight into the ground, under the dirt. That's the extent of your planning for after your death—the funeral. But really, isn't this a question worth looking into? Worth exploring? Worth giving five minutes of serious thought to? I get it. There are those out there who say the universe just formed out of a black hole and then appeared and evolved, and that people just live and die, going back into the ground from which we came. Let's remember that's from a strictly human perspective. I am not saying there is no such thing as evolution. That would be silly. There can be both a Creator and the concept of evolution. Why do you need just one or the other? We all grow and evolve. But there is also metamorphosis.

Butterflies start out their existence confined to a tree. They are confined to their ugly, sluggish bodies, until one day they turn into beautiful, multicolored butterflies. They don't evolve; they transform. I love the story of the dragonfly, a poem by Doris Stickney. A water bug, upset with everyone leaving and disappearing, vowed to tell the others where he went and why. He wakes up one day to find himself on a lily pad, transformed and transported to a beautiful place he could only know in his wildest dreams. Different now, he can spread his wings and see the magnificent glory that he couldn't have seen while trapped inside the body of a lowly water bug. The dragonfly poem is my favorite poem for funerals. It reminds me that there is more that we can't see or understand in our present reality. Just because we don't see it, or understand it, that doesn't make it *unreal*. We could all be lowly water bugs, just trying to make sense of this pool of water to which we are currently confined, trying to figure out where we are now, why we are here, and where we will go when we die (or transformed?). I wish we could know for sure. The poem ends with the dragonfly promising to return and tell his friends where he went and what had happened to the others. After the dragonfly begins to enjoy his newfound freedom, he remembers his friends trapped down below and made a beeline for them. But to his dismay, he cannot get there. He can see them. But because he is transformed, he is no longer a water bug, and he can no longer get down to the bottom of the water to tell his friends about where he went and why.

I am not saying evolution never takes place, but can't we be transformed, as well? Is that such a crazy thought—that the electrical activity within our great minds can be transformed? Even transformed into some new type of life? Some people I know scoff at such an idea. But open your mind. Open your thoughts to the possibility that there is more—beyond what we know. Science is not the end all, be all. It is just the beginning of knowledge. It is just the start. Evolution is just a theory. Some people take it as fact. Creationism is a theory, as well. But guess what: Both theories can coexist.

If you are going to spend an eternity somewhere, isn't it worth searching out where you might be, exploring the ideas, getting excited about the possibilities? I spent a month planning for a three-week vacation. Shouldn't a concern about eternity be worth more of your time? You only have four days left! Don't you want to know where you are going? If there is a Creator who made this awesome world, and who created our magnificent brains with the ability to form, grow, and learn, would He want your life to end so abruptly? What would be the purpose of that? Why would we ever learn anything? Why would we ever teach others? What would be the purpose for any of us to grow or learn? Were we just one grand experiment? A simulation? There would have to be a point, right? And if there is a Creator, He would have rules, right? I mean, think of the creators of video games. They care about their characters. They create good guys, and they create bad guys. But they also create rules.

If Someone created us, wouldn't they be rooting for us? Do you *really* think that if Someone took the time and effort to create us, He wound up the clock, let it go, and then forgot about us? It's possible, I suppose. I have had fish I bought and then forget to feed for days, maybe weeks. Maybe if I had a cat and it sat under my bed and never came out, I might forget about it. But I can tell you this: I *love* my dogs. They wait patiently for me as I go to work. They are so excited when I come back, and boy, am I excited to see them, too. I am excited to see my daughters, as well. But for sure, they are not as excited to see me at this time in their lives. I am more of a nuisance to them. I try to say hi, but they slam their bedroom doors closed. They are too busy to be with Mom. That makes me sad, but I know that one day, even if it's just for a few minutes, they will need me, they will show their love for me again, and of course, I still love them.

I don't know all the specifics, and I don't know how everything in the "afterlife" works. However, I do know I have loved things before. I have "created" two children, and I love them deeply. Even if I am busy at work, I never forget about them. So, although I don't know all the answers about the Creator's plans for you, I can ask you to think about these things. Search and seek out information. Plan. Don't just believe what your parents told you—or your teachers or your friends. Start your own search today. Remember, begin to live like you only have four more days left in your life. What would you want to know about where you might go after you leave this planet? If you were leaving on a long vacation, wouldn't you do some planning?

The problem is, most of us believe our final destination is so far in the future. We believe that we have fifty or seventy years left to start the planning process, so why should we start now and "waste" the time? "Play now, pay later," we typically say. But we don't know, do we? Every day is a gamble. Every day is a gift. Don't put it off. You could find yourself lost, or even worse, in a far worse place than here!

If I had never planned my three-week great Western vacation, I would have climbed into the driver's seat that day, unsure what direction to take. I would have been lost before I even started. And certainly, we would have never made it to our destinations. We would have never made it on time. We would have been too late, and we would have missed all the exciting things that were in store for us.

So, your homework for today is to start searching, to start planning. *But how?* you may ask. *How do I search for where I am going after I die? Especially if I am not sure what will happen? Where do I start?* There is no AAA available to help you answer these questions. Or is there? Is there a place to start? Yes, there is! There is a place to go. The Creator of the universe, the Creator of you, wants to get your attention and provide you with directions to your final destination. He has sought each of us out! I know what you are thinking: *Here it comes. Ugh! Here comes the "Jesus talk" to get shoved down my throat.* Nope. Not all. This is your journey, not mine. I have already made my decisions, and I am at peace with my upcoming final destination. I am here to help you find peace with *yours*.

This is your journey. I am just giving you information to think about and some options to consider. I am a trained social worker, and I wholeheartedly believe in free will and self-determination. So did our Creator. He will never *make* us love Him. That would not be true love; that would be control and coercion. And this leads us to the next question in the journey: If there is a Creator, and if there is an afterlife, an eternity to look forward to, how can we find it? The answer is that we must search for it. The Creator has attempted to contact us from the very beginning, or so we think. So, let's start there. Let's look at some of the facts. But then the next logical question would be, Which way is right?

Self-Reflection Questions

1. Do you care about where you may go in the afterlife?

2. Why do you care, or why not?

3. Where do you think you are you going in the afterlife?

4. Why do you think that is true?

5. How do you know you will eventually get there?

6. How can you find out more about the afterlife, and whether or not there is one?

7. What is something that stood out in the reading?

8. What are some more questions you have?

9. How can you learn more about it?

10. Now for the "if only" question: What would you have done differently today if you had known you'd be gone in four days?

CHAPTER 8

Which Way Is Right?

If our destiny is to end up somewhere, then there are different ways to get there, right? I mean, when we took our Western vacation, we could have traveled several ways. Our *ultimate* destination was the Grand Canyon. We could have gone the way we did, down to Texas and up from there. We could have gone across the northern states and come down from Utah, or we could have gone straight across the nation through Tornado Alley. There are many ways to get to the same destination, right? Well, yes and no.

We could have gotten to the Grand Canyon in a number of ways, that is true. But if I remember correctly, when we got close to the destination, there was only one winding, narrow dirt road that took us around to the western entrance. I remember this vividly because we got a ticket on that road for going too fast. I remember thinking there was no one else on the road, so what did it matter that we were speeding? However, the highway patrol officers patrolled it just the same. So, the answer to the question is that yes, we *could* have gotten to the general vicinity of the Grand Canyon by coming from any direction. But to get to the *west side entrance* of the Grand Canyon, we needed to travel *one particular road*. Why am I telling you this story?

I am telling you this story because if we are, indeed, from somewhere and that we were created and are, indeed, returning to somewhere, we need to examine this destination very thoroughly. This is probably the most important question of all. Because if we want to get to the right destination, we need to follow the directions exactly, or we will get lost. And if eternity is forever, we sure don't want to miss the boat or plane or whatever it is. We don't want to be lost forever!

I know, I get it. You may be thinking, *How can I get directions to know where I am going, when I don't actually know where I am going?* I get that. Really, I do. But let's think about this for a minute. If there really is a Creator, who designed us for purpose, for amazing things, wouldn't He have tried to provide us with the rules, give us directions, share the secrets, or guide us along the way of this crazy maze called life. Well, have there been any times in history when the Creator—or *Someone*—has tried to get ahold of us or give us a message? Yes, that has happened many times. Many people throughout history have claimed to have heard from God, the universe, or the Creator. Many messages have been given. But let's get back to the original question: Which way is right? I cannot answer that question for you. You have to decide that for yourself. But I can assure you that this question is one of significant importance. Most people don't think of it at all. They just answer it from a religious point of view. They state, "I am a Christian...," "a Catholic...," "Jewish...," "a Muslim...," and so on. I have heard this statement multiple times. I have also heard people say, "It doesn't matter, right? We are all worshiping one God, right? It's all the same God, right?" Well, that is both true and not true. I am not here to sway you one way or another. I have made my decision which way to go. I am only here to give you the options and choices, and you need to decide which makes the most sense for you. But I can tell you with 100 percent certainty it *may* be the same God whom everyone worships, but the rules are different on how we will get to the eternal destination that we all seek. You don't have to like the rules, and you don't have to like me or agree with me; I am only here to tell you about the rules and choices, so you have the correct knowledge. Not all roads lead to eternity, according to the different messages. And if you only have three more days to live now, you will likely put extremely high importance on choosing the correct answer to this one huge question.

There are a myriad of choices to choose from. I think the last I looked, there were over four thousand different religions from which we could choose. It is daunting, to say the least. I get it. I mean, decisions, decisions, right? How can you be sure you are choosing the right path, the right way? It doesn't seem fair. I know—I get it. It wasn't fair that I got a ticket on that winding dirt road to the Grand Canyon, but I did. I didn't make the rules, and I didn't create the road. I didn't draw the map. My job is to just follow the directions and the rules.

With that being said, plenty of people have claimed to have the directions to heaven and eternal life. Let's just take a look at the main ones. From these primary ideas, the different religions spread out like wildfire, like sprouts or weeds, and it becomes hard to see the jungle through the trees. So, let's unravel some of the weeds, to see more of a clear path. There are three primary monotheistic faiths. (*Monotheistic* means "following one God.") So that means, there are three religions out there that demand complete devotion to just one God. No idols are allowed.

I am being very simplistic here, but research has shown the average person can't even pass a test on the basic tenets of *their own faith*. I was one of those people, hence the start of my own spiritual journey. I was a thirty-year-old self-proclaimed Christian, and I didn't even know the Christian beliefs myself. I thought I was just supposed to be a good person. But that was not the right rule—hence, my breakdown.

The reason people don't know much about their own religion probably has a lot to do with religious faith being taking out of the schools and history books. Many people have no idea what even half the world is fighting about. In my world cultures class in eleventh or twelfth grade, I remember hearing all about the Middle East being the hotspot of the world's greatest conflict. But really, until a few years ago, I had no idea why. I am not trying to jam anything down your throat, but I am here to give you the facts, which you can look up in any history book. My point is, if you consider that we might have a Creator and that that Creator has tried to give us rules and guidelines, then these are the three primary religions on which you would want to focus, the deities that have attempted to contact us. Yes, these all start with one God, and they all branch off from there. Again, this is your decision what to believe—I am just giving you the basics from which to choose.

Here is a very brief summary: Abraham was an old man who lived six thousand years ago in Israel. He claimed he had an encounter with the Creator of the universe and was told that he and his wife, Sarah, would have as many descendants as there were stars in the sky, and that they would inherit the Promised Land (found in today's Middle East). When Abraham heard

IF ONLY?

this, he laughed, because his wife was one hundred years old at that time. They didn't believe what God had said. I wouldn't have, either. They waited, and waited, and waited—and nothing. It reminds me of my daughters at Christmas. I get them their favorite outfit at the store when we see it there. But they can't wait two more weeks until Christmas comes until it's under the tree. They have to take matters into their own hands and buy the same outfit I had just bought and wrapped up for them. Well, Abraham was no different. Like a child at Christmastime, he couldn't wait; he and Sarah didn't trust God's process. They took matters into their own hands. They used Sarah's servant as a surrogate, and out came Ishmael, Abraham's firstborn son. But guess what, Sarah eventually did get pregnant, and out came Isaac. Well, now there was a conundrum. The Maker of the universe had said the firstborn would receive the inheritance. So, who was truly the firstborn? Ishmael or Isaac? I am not sure if you know this, but the nations of the world are still fighting over that simple question, six thousand years later! They are still fighting over that little strip of *"Promised* Land." Is this just a story somebody made up, like you might have believed? Maybe? But the whole world is still fighting over *that very question*. It should make you wonder, or at least question, that someone for sure must have witnessed something great. Someone was promised a piece of land by the

Creator, and they are still fighting over that one little piece of real estate today.

Okay, so in a nutshell, those are the two basic monothetic faiths: The descendants of Isaac became Israel, which practices the Jewish faith, and the descendants of Ishmael are Islam's Muslims, who believe Ishmael was the chosen one and that the land belongs to the Palestinians. The Palestinians believe that Israel and the Jewish people stole their land. I know I promised not to jam Jesus down your throat, but where does He fit in to all this? Well, Isaac's descendants grew so great and so fast (like the "stars in the sky") that the rulers were threatened by them. They were made into slaves, and they needed someone to rescue them out of Egypt (hence the story of Moses). Moses freed them and with God's guidance and protection, brought them to the Promised Land (the very land in the Middle East that everyone is still fighting over). However, with the rise and fall of Jerusalem over the years (depending on whether the Israelites followed their God's rules or not), it was promised that a Savior would come, Someone who would save them from the enemy (literal enemies in this physical earth, and our true enemy, in the spiritual realm). Thus, Jesus enters the scene on a white horse, as promised. Well, not so fast. They were promised a Savior, a mighty Deliverer. What they got instead was an infant in a manger. There was nothing supernatural about

Him—or so the Jewish people thought. Jesus lived His life, and He started teaching and performing miracles at the age of thirty—until He was thirty-three. Then the same people who had looked for Him, who had longed for Him, crucified Him for being blasphemous (or lying). I mean, He was making outrageous claims that He was the literal Son of God. They would not put up with such mockery of their God, and they put Him to death. However, after Jesus was crucified and buried, *He rose again.* He had told those around Him that He would be back again one day, and that they should tell others the Good News—that death had been defeated, and an eternal life in heaven was now possible. Christians believe that Jesus was sent by God to tell us more about the Creator of the universe, how He loves us and wants to save us all from eternal death. Jesus claimed that He was the only way to heaven. No one is worthy to go to heaven without His help. None of us is good enough. We have all sinned and fallen short of the Creator's glory.

Now, this is where I often lose people. People like to say that these are all stories. Maybe, but these "stories" have withstood the test of time. How many stories do you know that have lasted six thousand years or more? Some people say that the oral traditions, which is how these stories were passed down through the generations, are like the game where you whisper in one person's ear and the story eventually gets twisted. Still other people say that the Bible was written by mere men. Yes, it was; that is true. It was written by men who believed that what they saw was true. Now, if you believe in a Creator, you must choose one of these three main stories, especially if you want to please the Creator and worship Him. Each of these faiths believe they are worshiping the one true God.

If you want to go to heaven and have eternal life, the rules are different for each of these faiths, in case you didn't know. Whether you believe in Jesus or not, He is the One who stated the rules. Don't kill the messenger. I didn't make the rules; I am just giving you the facts. You can argue if they are, in fact, the facts, but again, I am just the messenger, telling you what Jesus has said the facts are. There are many witnesses who say that Jesus is the Son of God, the Creator, and Jesus told them there is only one way to heaven. And that is faith. It has nothing to do with how good of a person you are, because none of us is worthy. None. Again, I didn't make the rules. I am just giving you the information. Jesus is the only ticket out of this world and into the next. You either accept this, or you don't.

Now, some of you may believe that Jesus is scrunching His nose at you if you choose not to follow Him. However, if you have a clear understanding, that is not what He is saying. He is saying that something went awry after the creation of the earth (when sin entered), our "computers" are now crashing. The hard drive is failing, and we can cash it in for a new life or not. I'm sorry, the virus has infected us all, and it is eventually going to crash. He has paid the price for your warranty. Accept it or don't—it's your choice. He can't force you to take His free gift. That's your choice.

Now, again, I am not trying to jam Jesus down your throat; I am just giving you the facts about the rules. If you don't believe me, that is okay. My goal here is to get you to explore, to read more about all of this. Don't believe me on my own word. Search out the truth for yourself. You want to know the rules, right? You only have three days left!

These are the three main religions. The Jewish people are still waiting for a savior. Muslims believe Ishmael was the chosen one and that you get to Paradise by practicing a series of religious behaviors. Islam is all about good works. Christians, on the other hand, believe Jesus paid the price to save us from our sins. God so loved the world He created, that He sent His only Son to us to help us and to save us (see John 3:16). Jesus paid the price for our sins. It doesn't matter how good you are, your good deeds don't get you to heaven. Believing and accepting this gift is the only way. Jewish people do not believe Jesus was the Messiah, although there are some "Messianic Jews" who do. Why do they believe and other Jews do not? It is often because they are unaware of Isaiah 53, which is a "forbidden" chapter of the Jewish *Tanakh*. They are still waiting for their promised messiah, even though, for those of you who like math and statistical calculations and mathematics, professor Peter Stoner found that the chances of Jesus fulfilling only *eight* of prophecies in the Old Testament (there are far more than eight!) by sheer chance is 1 in 100,000,000,000,000.

The theologian C.S Lewis once pointed out that although Jesus is labeled as one of the great moral teachers of all time, the outrageous claims that Jesus made about being the Son of God would actually make Him one of only three things: 1) He was the Son of God; 2) He was completely insane; or 3) He was truly evil. It had to be one of those three things; He could not be all three, and He could not be anything else. We must believe one of them as true because there is plenty of historical proof, outside of the Bible, and in history books, that Jesus was a real person who lived and walked the earth.

So, why do so many people believe that Jesus was the Savior and not just some schizophrenic walking around? It is because He returned to the people who followed Him (His disciples) and showed Himself to them after He had been dead for three days. Now, what is interesting is that these same disciples are the ones who had run away and hid themselves just three days before. They didn't want to be killed—not even for Jesus. To them, He was a cool guy and everything, but none of them were willing to die for Him at that time. It was *only after He was raised from the dead that each of them* had an awakening—and that awakening was so strong that *nearly every single one of them* died a gruesome death rather than refuse to deny the truth that they had seen Jesus raised from the dead. That was the game changer for me. In addition, *five hundred* other people also gave accounts of seeing Him after His resurrection.

Now again, take away the Bible if you do not believe it is true, but there are history books that do talk about Jesus and His disciples, who were killed. What other religion claims that their leader died and was raised back to life? Again, I am not telling you which religion to believe; I am just trying to interest you in the topic, so that you go and explore for yourself. If you only have three days left to live, wouldn't you want to know where you are going after you die, and the exact way to get there? Don't you want the golden ticket—if there is one? What if there is only one way? Do you want to take the chance of missing it by not even exploring that fact?

If you only had three days to live, would you take that chance? People can laugh and joke about hell, but I bet you would not be laughing if you only had three days left to make a decision that could alter where you might spend eternity. People also talk very vaguely about heaven, and many people picture it as a place with angels strumming harps while sitting on clouds. But what if there is an *actual place* where our souls are transported after death. What if there is an *actual place* where our "electricity" travels to? The first law of thermodynamics is that energy can neither be created or destroyed. In essence, it can only be converted to one form to another. So, where does our "energy" go after death? Do we really have a soul? Some people may think about reincarnation at this point. But Jesus doesn't say that is what happens—He tells us that each of us will live eternally, in a different place from planet earth, where we live our current lives.

Another important thing to think of is this: If one of the Gods in these three faiths is the correct one to follow, wouldn't He have given us a specific guide for living life that would make our lives easier—that would make Him easier to find? And if so, wouldn't you want to read it. Research tells us that even today, in our modern times, the Bible is still the most popular book in the world. The average American home has seven Bibles in it! However, the Bible is also one of the least-read books. Wouldn't it be a shame if you had a map to keep you from getting lost on the way to heaven but you never picked it up to read it the whole time you were here on the earth? Maybe there is a reason the "BIBLE" has been nicknamed the "Book of Instructions Before Leaving Earth"!

So, what about all the other religions besides the three monotheistic ones we've discussed? Well, they are multiple. In a nutshell, they are polytheistic, meaning they believe in and worship *many different* gods. Many Eastern religions worship the sun, the trees, the ground, different animals, and so on. Some religions even worship human beings themselves. My challenge to you is to ask yourself this question: If you were a Creator, would you want your creation to be worshiped, or yourself? I am trying to not be judgmental here; I am just asking you to think about that question. Let me try to explain it another way: If you have a child and they draw an amazing picture for you, of course, you would admire it, frame it, and adore it. But wouldn't your actual *praise* go to the child who made it, the one who created the picture? These are just my thoughts for you to consider and ponder.

There are too many other religions to discuss, and this is not the purpose of the book. Thousands of them are offshoots of the three primary religions. Many of them claim to have heard from God, and they give messages that either add to the Bible or change things that the Bible says are true. However, it is important to be very careful about following other versions of the Holy Word.

The original Bible is a collection of many writings. It was written by multiple people claiming to have seen, or been given, the very Word of God to write down. Each person wrote a story from their own perspective of what they saw happen with their own eyes, or what they heard with their own ears. They claim these words, rules, and guidelines were inspired by the Creator, or His Holy Spirit. The original Bible has gone through a highly scrutinized peer-review process to make sure that all the writings in it are consistent with each other. That is why it is important to be careful of following rules or guidelines outside the original text. It is of dire importance to choose the right text to follow. *You want to have the right map.*

On the other hand, if you never pick any of them up to read, you will never know which one is right. They all give you different guidelines or rules for you to get to heaven. But which one makes the most sense? My goal, again, here is just to get you to think more closely about these issues. Your (eternal) life may literally depend on it. You are running out of time! What if hell is a real place?

Self-Reflection Questions

1. Do you follow any particular faith?

2. Do you know the actual beliefs of your faith—not just a vague, general idea, but the actual rules on how to get to eternity, if there is one?

3. Would you like to learn more about other faiths?

4. Have you ever researched the different faiths to understand their differences?

5. How can you learn and find out more about them?

6. If there is a guidebook, or map, on how to live your life here on earth, would you want to read it? Why or why not?

7. What, if anything, is stopping you?

8. What is something that stood out in the reading?

9. What are some more questions you have?

10. Now for the "if only" question: What would you have done differently today if you had known you'd be gone in three days?

CHAPTER 9

When Is It Time?

My memory is horrible. Old age, I guess. Or it could be that I am just crazy-busy, or perhaps my mind is filled with fog because of all the carbs I eat. But one thing I can remember vividly in college is sitting on the edge of my bed in my dorm room with my roommate. We were talking at length about the concept of time. No, I was not smoking pot, as some of you may think. We were just pondering the concept. How such a simple word—*time*—could determine the fate of the rest of our lives. For example, at the time, I was dating someone I had met at a party. I don't remember the specific details of the party, but I do remember the police were called, and everyone scrambled to leave. As I passed this one particular boy in the narrow hallway of the apartment complex, our eyes locked, and he asked where I was going. Long story short, we went on to date for several months. It did not turn out to be anything special, but my point is, those few seconds, the timing of the call to the cops, and the exact movement of the people in the hallway, determined the course of the next few months of my life. And if you think about it, it may have even changed the course of my entire life. No, I didn't end up with him in the long term. But for those few months, my lack of availability "on the market," the people I didn't meet, determined the timing of my next encounter, which allowed me to meet my husband. Each encounter I had impacted the next.

Take a few minutes to think about that. Certain moments in time will determine the future of everything else. Anyone who has seen the movie *The Butterfly Effect*, in which one action of a character has a ripple effect on the future, or the movie *Sliding Doors*, in which two paths collide, can see the outcome of this. In *Sliding Doors*, the outcome of the character's life was portrayed in two separate stories of what could have happened to her, depending on whether or not she caught the train that day.

Think of your life and where you are at, the people you have met, the times when you were at the exact right place at the right time. Time is a critical factor in what determines the course of your fate. Your very existence is because of time. It is like a domino effect.

Think about the Twin Towers. There are many stories of people who were stuck in traffic or who were just a few minutes late to work that day, September 11, 2001. Those few minutes determined the course of their lives—their very fate.

We are also slaves to time. We set the alarm to get up on time for work. We only have so much time to get certain things done. We come home and have to cook for our kids in time for them to go to sports practice. We have to be in bed by a certain time to get enough sleep for the next day. The clock keeps turning, over and over and over again. Time never stops. Even when we are on vacation, the clock keeps ticking. There is some respite, but there is still no stopping the time from passing by. It continues, whether you like it or not. Our children grow up before our very eyes, and we scream at time to "just stop turning!" We want to enjoy those smiles and giggles just one more day. Then it happens. You're not sure how or why, but your children don't giggle as much, your hair is gray, you've gained weight, and wrinkles have set in. And there they are, those dreaded silver threads in your hair. A testament of how much time truly has gone by.

Time is our worst enemy. How many books and techniques have been written about how to save time? Better time management saves money and gives us more free time. But of course, the more you have of it, the more you fill it with more wasted time. We try to prioritize our time, but it just never feels like enough. Our lack of time feels like a bottomless pit in which we keep spinning around. Like an hourglass, we are just swirls of sand, destined to be squeezed down the little funnel

WHEN IS IT TIME?

one day. We can't stop it. It has gravity. It pulls us. Pressures us. We try to resist, but there is no stopping it. There is no escape. We will all be sucked down to the other side one day. Who can save us?

Let's first look at the concept of time. What is it? The dictionary states that time "is an indefinite continued progress of existence and events that occur in an apparently irreversible succession." Did you ever feel that time is going faster and faster? Research says that's because of our neural connections. For example, do you remember the feeling when you were little that life seemed to last forever and that summer break from school was a lifetime? Researchers says that time is perception. Now, I know it is real, right? Sixty minutes equals an hour. That is a scientific fact. However, my perception of those sixty minutes seemed longer when I was younger. Why? Some researchers say it was because everything was new. So, when I was five and there was a summer break, it was a new experience for me. My neural connections were just forming. Now that my neural connections are established, and after doing the same thing over and over, the connections are faster and faster. Therefore, time is perceived to go faster. So does Christmas. It seems to come sooner every year. It seems that the time between Christmas each year feels more like one month than twelve. No wonder older people keep up their Christmas trees throughout the year. What is the sense of taking it down when the months go by so fast? Another interesting fact I learned is that in order to feel like time is slowing down, you need to make new memories. In this way, you will be creating new neural connections. So, with that being said, my point is that even time is perception and can be an illusion.

There is no denying, however, that in whatever faith you believe or what kind of scientist you are, the world is like one big, wound-up clock. It is turning, accelerating, growing, and advancing. However, everything that grows eventually breaks down and dies. And so will you. I know that is an anxiety-producing fact for many of you. And rather than face your fears, like most people, you would prefer to avoid it. It seems safer. As a psychologist, I can understand that. I see this every day—it is what anxiety disorders and phobias are made of. Avoidance feels good initially. It makes you feel good and safe. However, anxiety is like a monster that grows and then dominates and controls you. To conquer it, you have to get out there and face your fears. You have to expose yourself to the gremlin. He isn't so bad. But the more you hide, the more control he will have, and the more anxiety you will experience. Gradual exposure is the answer in many cases.

I will give you an example. I was shy in high school. No one would have ever imagined me as a college professor. But yet I faced my fears of speaking in front of others. Against all odds, I became a public speaker, and now I love it. Okay, maybe I don't love talking to large audiences, but I definitely enjoy teaching. It has been one of the most favorite jobs I ever had. Who knew? If I hadn't gotten out of my comfort zone, challenged myself, and addressed my worst fears, I would have never known that I could do it.

Don't let time be your enemy. Let it become your friend. Instead of letting it produce anxiety, let it be motivating. Let it be inspirational. Let it be your coach. Let it push you toward great things.

How can you do that? Think of the greater picture. I know this is the opposite of what we are all told. We are often told to take things one step at a time, one day at a time. That can be helpful in some situations. But if we were lost in a jungle, stumbling through the overgrowth, moving step by step would take forever. The path could be two feet away from us, and we would miss it because we didn't have the big picture! We need both.

If you were lost, only to find out later that you should have turned left and that the exit was right there, you would have been angry with yourself if you didn't find it. Certain tasks need to be broken down to make them more manageable—but don't miss the big picture, either. Don't miss the big picture of *time*. It can be your friend in finding happiness. It is essential in finding your purpose. Unless you have a big picture of time, you are only performing meaningless tasks.

For example, consider that I hire someone to mow my grass and they only have an hour to spend on the task. What if they spent all that time mowing my front yard, when really I needed the back of the yard cut because I was planning a picnic? They would have been frustrated that they had wasted their time, and I would have been upset too. I have done that myself. I have cleaned my house before picnics, only to realize that no one ever stepped foot in the rooms inside the house. If only I had known what I didn't know at the time, I wouldn't have wasted my time. In essence, the big picture of time is needed. It helps us with purpose.

The earth keeps rotating. What is the big picture? It reminds me of the great, wise words of King Solomon. He compares the pursuit of much of what we do in seeking pleasure as useless and meaningless, as if we are just chasing the wind. It feels like that is true sometimes, for sure. The world just keeps spinning around and around, and we can't get off the hamster wheel. We can't even get up for a breath of fresh air. So, try to look at the big picture instead. Consider questions such as where we are, why we are here, how we got here, and where we are going. If you keep avoiding these questions because of your lack of time, your work, or your daily pleasures, you will miss the big picture. You have to think about it. It is your friend. It will get you out of the jungle quicker and easier.

Generations pass, only to be forgotten. Of course, some historical figures stand out. However, most of us die, only to be forgotten. Think about it. Seriously, do you remember your great-great grandparents? What a wonderful life they may have lived. I know it's hard to think about, but each of them had a life, worries, fun experiences, dreams, fears, hopes, and challenges. But do you ever think about them? I think of my 102-year-old nana often. As a matter of fact, I am sitting outside right now, looking at the swing on my back porch, remembering the time a year ago when she was sitting there. She expressed how beautiful the view was and commented that I should write a book out there on the swing. She is still alive, but I look at the bench now, thinking that one day she will be gone. She will be no more. Forgotten. Not by me or my kids, but their kids will never know her. Maybe they will glance at her picture, or even study it for a few minutes. But all they will have is a picture that stopped time for a moment and saved it. Without that picture, she will be forgotten by the next generation. Certainly, she will be on a family tree, and people will want to know her name and her lineage. But she will only be a name—the name of a person who was here and then was no more. What is the point of that?

Well, the point is, I guess, to learn and to impact others. For example, those words Nana spoke in that space and time changed the course of my life. I am writing that book. It is this book you are holding, that I wrote to help others to find their purpose. Maybe that is the point. We try to find meaning and purpose in our lives, but it does all come down to time. Each of us only has so much time. You may have a hundred years or three days left—I don't know—but if you don't use the time you have wisely, it will be wasted. And if there is a Creator, you will have disappointed both Him and yourself that you wasted it on the silly things. That's not to say there isn't a time for fun experiences but think of the concept of time. It is your very life. We all come into this world alone, and we will go out alone. Don't depend on anyone else for where you will spend eternity.

And, by the way, the clock is ticking—two more days! I think now is the time to get your priorities straight!

Self-Reflection Questions

1. What is your perception of time like?

2. How do you spend your time?

3. Do you ever feel like you have enough time? Why or why not?

4. If there is a Creator and He came back, would you be proud to share with Him how you have spent your time?

5. What would you like to do in the time you have left on this earth?

6. How can you make new memories in order to slow down time?

7. What is something that stood out in the reading?

IF ONLY?

8. What are some more questions you have?

9. How can you learn more?

10. Now for the "if only" question: What would you have done differently today if you had known you'd be gone in two days?

CHAPTER 10

Whose Responsibility Is It?

I remember when I was pregnant. It felt like such a miracle. I couldn't wait to bring this little bundle of joy into the world. I waited and waited and waited with anticipation. I didn't know it at the time, but I was having a girl. I mean, I knew I had made something incredible. I went to all the doctor appointments to make sure she was healthy, and I made sure I was eating right. I even used a little contraption to try to hear her little heartbeat through my stomach. I would get excited to feel her every kick. It was a long nine months, which felt like forever, but yet it was still one of the best times of my life.

My husband and I had created a little miracle, and I couldn't wait to meet her or him. I thought about my baby each and every day. Of course, some days I was frustrated with the growing pains. I mean, the big belly, the stretch marks, and the feelings of nausea that she brought on were no fun, for sure. But I loved her, and I knew it would all be worth it just to see her one day in the not-so-distant future. It was just a matter of time. It sure felt like a long time, but in the scope of a lifetime, nine months really wasn't that long at all.

I had another daughter several years later. I loved her just the same. I couldn't wait for her arrival. She was created, loved, and worth waiting for. Still, today, even though they drive me crazy, both of my girls are loved so much, despite all their shortcomings, as well as my own. But both of them came into this world alone. Each of them has her own personality. They are both so different, despite having the same parents and growing up in the same home. I am often in awe at their differences. How can it be? One likes to get up early in the morning, and one likes to stay up late. One likes fruits and not vegetables; one likes vegetables and not fruit. One was born with blue eyes and one with brown eyes. One of them was the tallest in preschool; the other was one of the tiniest. Each of them is so different, despite being loved the same way and created by the same two people. They are different because they come into the world different. They will both go out different, as well. They will have different experiences, different loves, different careers, different challenges, and different successes. But they are both loved in the same way. You, too, are loved. Again, I can't tell you to believe in a Creator. But after everything you have thought about in the past ten days, doesn't the possibility or probability of a Creator make more sense? If there is a Creator, then you are loved. Just as I anxiously awaited my children, knowing they would be filled with both good and bad, I loved them, if Someone is waiting on the other side for you, what will it be like when you arrive there? What have you learned? Will your life have been meaningful, worthwhile? Have you loved and helped others? I am sure the Creator will love you, no matter what happened in your life here on earth. But you come in this world alone to meet your parents, and you will go out alone into the great unknown by yourself, to meet Whoever is on the other side. How great it will be if there is Someone there to greet you, but will you be healthy—and I mean, psychologically, emotionally, spiritually healthy?

In this life, it is all physical, right? I awaited my children's physical birth, hoping and praying they each had ten fingers and ten toes, a healthy, beating heart, and an intact brain. I know there are people who are not as lucky. They give birth to children with struggles and physical disabilities. But still, those children are loved by their parents or caretakers. There is learning somewhere in that experience, whether it be patience or unconditional love. In the next world, if there is a Creator, will it be a spiritual birth, and what are the expectations of the Creator for when we arrive? Maybe it is similar to how we send our kids to school and then look forward to their return, to hear about all they have learned. Does the Creator anxiously await our arrival, to hear of all we have learned and the knowledge we have gained in this world? Will He want to know how we grew and matured? How we developed emotionally and spiritually?

We come into this world alone, and we will go out alone. Yes, sometimes there are twins or even quadruplets or more, but we all will answer alone. We are all different with different abilities, knowledge, and skills given to us or acquired, as well as different experiences. You can only account for yourself, so it is your decision.

You have a free will. You can decide what you want to learn in this life through your struggles, losses, pleasure, and pain. You are growing, and what you learn or take from your life is up to you. Nobody can make you change or see things a different way. Only you have the power to do that. Others can guide you, but it is ultimately up to you what choices you make.

The great question is, do you want to consider the possibility of something more and seek it out? Don't depend on others. Seek it out for yourself. I know no one has the answers. Remember that not even scientists have all the answers. Don't depend entirely on them, either. They only know what they know now in this moment in time.

WHOSE RESPONSIBILITY IS IT?

For example, the idea of a God knowing all our thoughts and seeing everything seemed impossible years ago. Some of you may still think it seems impossible. But think about how much we know now about computers and technology and tracking devices. Do you not think that a Creator, much more advanced than us, could do all the things He claims to do? What seemed outrageous years ago now seems more and more plausible as time goes by. Maybe we need to trust Someone who knows much more than we do for the answers. We only know what we know at the moment. If only we would have listened more closely, seen more vividly, and understood more fully.

Remember, when I was told my father was going to die, I didn't understand it fully. But I was told. What if you have been told the answers? Take some time to really see and listen—but not with your physical eyes and ears. Look and listen with your spiritual eyes and ears.

This makes me think of all the things I can't see with my physical eyes. When I call someone on the phone, there is usually someone on the other line, even though I can't see the actual signal that takes place and I don't know or understand how it works for the message scientifically to get to them and then back to me. It is all invisible. But nevertheless, it is there.

As a psychologist, I have to participate in behavioral observations in schools sometimes. I was observing one particular student in his computer technology classroom not long ago. The teacher was discussing wireless networks and how they work. While I felt lost in the discussion of all the intricate details of the workings of the internet, what stood out to me was also the actual simplicity of it all. WIFI is just a wireless network that uses radio waves that connect to each other. Radios, televisions, and cell phones all do the same thing. My humble, very limited understanding of it all is that it is a lot like a two-way communication system. Data is transmitted, downloaded, and decoded using adapters and routers. That is the limit of my understanding! But think of that for just one second. If we understand that as a simple process, is it so crazy to consider the possibility of communicating with our Creator in many of the same ways, even if He is far away? If our brains (which computers are very much modeled after) are part electricity, is it so unimaginable to consider that we could have some sort of communication with God? Could God in heaven (wherever that is) have some sort of invisible type of network that we cannot physically see, but that allows us to have access to Him on a daily basis? In a sense, could there be some type of system in which He can download things to us, and we can upload our prayers?

This reminds me of my college days. When I had to call home, we had to use phones that were connected to the walls. I could only hear my mom's voice, not see her face. Now, I can FaceTime my daughter while she is at away at college, and it's like I am right there with her! How far we have come in such a short time. Maybe that is why Jesus told us He is with us always. We don't understand what that means right now. We only know what we know at this time.

God tells us to pray constantly. Maybe that is why prayer works. Could we be using some sort of two-way communication system when we pray? Think of multiple prayers. Could they be giving more invisible signals to the main system, making it more powerful than just one person's prayer? I know that if I get multiple messages at work about the same thing, it gets my attention more so than just one message. Just some food for thought. Also think about how in the Bible, God says we are a new creature when we believe and trust in Him. Could we then be hooked up to some special system that helps to change our thoughts and feelings? Perhaps it downloads special information if we choose to follow Him, similar to how we upload special software programs or virus protection in our computers. Is it so crazy to dismiss the idea that we could communicate with God on some level? Maybe we just do not understand it all yet.

How exciting it is that every day we learn more information that increases our understanding just a little bit more. And yet, we could be light-years behind in understanding all that our Creator has in store for our use in the future. If only…if only we would just trust in something greater than ourselves.

I want to be very careful here. I do not want to reduce God to some kind of computer network just because that is only what we understand at this point in time. But I am trying to illustrate the point of how much more we know now than we did a thousand years ago—even less than a hundred years ago! Imagine what the Creator of the universe knows. He tells us that He created the earth in a breath, and He can destroy it in a breath. We may not understand that now, but maybe a few hundred years from now, we will be closer to understanding. In the meantime, it demonstrates the point that just because we cannot see something, that does not make it unreal. We still have a lot to learn. That understanding is of the utmost importance. Just because we cannot see God, that does not make Him unreal. We have to trust Him.

Here is another word of caution. If there is a way to communicate with a higher power out there, or God, could there also be way for the reception to be intercepted? I think we all want to be sure we are speaking to the "right" Creator. Many evil people on the internet are deceptive. Pedophiles and sex traffickers pretend to be people they are not in order to prey on innocent victims and lure them in. The Bible does say that Satan is like a wolf in sheep's clothing (see Matthew 7:15). Things that could look innocent or alluring could be intercepting and mimicking the Creator's will for your life. It is frightening to think that someone else could be preying on us if we do not know the correct voice of our true Creator. If we do not read His Word, or His directions, we could be easily led astray.

Returning to the jungle story, you would not want to go farther into the jungle; you want to get out safely. You do not want to be stuck in the jungle forever and live alone with regret. One of the most important things to do is to make sure you are following the right directions. That means choosing the correct voice to follow, and then following the right path. You do not want to be deceived.

We discussed in an earlier chapter about making the right choice. Think about which path seems to make the most sense. Think of the bigger picture. Then spread your wings and fly. Search, looking everywhere for the truth. Seek it, and you will find it. Just like if you do not turn on the radio, you won't get a clear station or hear any sound, if you do not turn on your spiritual radio and seek the true Creator, how will you ever find Him? I don't claim to know much about anything, but I do understand the fundamentals of communication. The first thing to do to communicate with someone effectively is to reach out.

The other important factor is to make sure you are talking with the right Creator, not an imposter who is trying to hijack you and your life. The Creator of the Bible does tell us there is a spiritual dimension beyond our understanding. There is also a lion looking for someone to devour (see 1 Peter 5:8). We need to be alert and vigilant that we are not tricked by him in any way.

The Bible also warns us that Satan, our enemy, wants to be like God and will try to mimic Him (see Isaiah 14:13–14). We need to be careful of this in regard to all the technological advancements we have made. It could be easy to start thinking we do not need a Creator because we can do everything ourselves. Cloning things, altering DNA, or anything like that may be close to playing the part of God. I am not saying that technology and new inventions cannot be helpful, but again, we want to be mindful of that. Pride often comes before a fall (see Proverbs 16:18).

It is frightening that some people will eventually think we do not need to know God or go to heaven, because we will have the ability to live here on earth forever. Because we don't know what else is out there, the allure of having it all here could be tempting. The idea of transplanting our brains into artificial bodies is not far off. Why would we want to go back to where we came from (heaven, with God) if we could figure out how to live forever here? Why would we need God if we could figure out these secrets? That is a sad thought. God warns us there is a great deceiver who will perform many miracles and try to be like Him (see Mark 13:22; Revelation 13:11–14).

We need God to escape what will come in the future. He knows what happens in the end. I don't know how, but He claims He does. Again, we don't know what we don't know. I am sure in two hundred years, we will understand more about time travel. But right now, we don't know what we don't know. Again, we just have to trust and accept it for what it is.

I warn my daughters all the time about the consequences of social media. I tell them about all the opportunities for deception out there. If they do not heed my warning, they could be led astray; worst-case scenario, they could be kidnapped. I would give my life for a ransom for them, to get them back. That is what our Creator has said to us. He is basically saying that someone has hijacked us, stolen us away from Him. We are on the wrong road, destined to follow the path to destruction. In essence, we are lost in the vast jungle. He has paid the ransom for us to return home to Him. There is no other way to get there. There is nothing we can do to get ourselves out of this mess. If we don't accept that, there is no coming home. He didn't put us there. We put ourselves there, because we did not follow the right directions. But even if my children did not follow my directions, I for sure would want them back. I would not want them to be captured and tortured forever. I would want them back home, safe with me. However, it is also true that if my eighteen-year-old has run away, I cannot *make* her come home if she doesn't want to. The Creator can only try to help you. You must choose to accept that help—or not.

This makes me think about why God had to die to pay our ransom. I do not fully understand it myself, but if you follow the teachings of the Bible, it tells you that the wages of sin are death (see Romans 6:23). That is the consequence for our sin. We are all susceptible to infection for some reason. That makes me think of a computer I had several years ago. I didn't want to pay for the virus protection when my free trial ran out. And of course, a few months later a virus crashed my computer. I was so angry that I didn't listen to the advice that told me to get the protection. Just one wrong click, and my entire system was infected. It wasn't my fault. But viruses are out there. All of our computers are susceptible. And contracting that virus was the consequence of my not using the protective software. I was now exposed to hackers and all sort of things on my hard drive that I do not pretend to understand. But I was told beforehand the consequences of not having the protection and that the computer was at risk.

I also think another reason God died to pay our ransom is that maybe we wouldn't have believed it if others did not see Him in the flesh and had witnesses to tell us about all that He had done for us and seen it with their own two eyes. Maybe He had to die, or we would be stuck here in the world forever, not seeing or believing any of it. The Bible says that the Word became flesh (see John 1:14). The written word was brought to life. Words have more power when we can physically see something. But if we do not look, we cannot see. If we are not prepared or we are unaware of the warnings in the written word, how will we escape the consequences of following the wrong directions? If there is a Creator, we need to trust that He alone knows all the answers. He has given us a map, directions, and warnings of what to look out for and what not to do. He does not want us to crash and burn. He wants us to have the protection program. However, we must also be careful not to change the rules. But again, if we do not read the map for ourselves, anyone could tell us what it says and we would be misled. It is important to read the map for ourselves. It is absolutely our responsibility to do that.

It is also our responsibility to make the call. If you want to communicate with someone, you have to pick up the phone. You have to call, text, or even email. You will usually get a response. The other person might not answer right away, or they may be busy, but it is still part of your responsibility to reach out and make the call. It is also your responsibility to answer the phone if someone is trying to call you. If you do not take the time to do that, you may miss the information. Communication is important. I have a friend who never picks up her phone. She has missed many opportunities in her life because of that.

You may ask, How could a Creator care personally about each one of us? There are just too many people on the earth, right? I get that feeling when I travel on an airplane, and I look down at how small everything is. We are like ants—smaller than ants, in the universe. I could tread on ants. I don't think one iota about ants. But heck, I sure do notice and think of them when there is a multitude of them in my kitchen. That gets my attention. Or the one cricket in my yard that makes the loudest noise. It gets my attention.

My point is this: It is your responsibility to seek out the Creator, to get His attention, or at the very least, to have a great multitude try to get the attention of the Creator for you. But if you do not attempt to do something, how will you ever know? If you are unsure that is okay, just make the call, make the noise, knock on the doors. Don't do nothing. This is your life. You can't blame anyone else if you don't make the effort. Sometimes you have to make multiple calls until you get through. For whatever reason, sometimes the message doesn't get through. Sometimes someone is away from the desk for a while, or the message gets lost in the shuffle. Sometimes calling several times or saying it is urgent gets the message across.

We do not understand what goes on in the spiritual realm. Just as my dogs could have no true understanding of what I actually do at work all day, I must also acknowledge the fact that I have no idea what our Creator is doing on a daily basis. I would think heaven is perhaps more interesting than just an angel sitting on a cloud all day playing a harp. Not to mention that I am sure my perception of time is much different than His. Years could really be seconds in His mind.

That reminds me of when I was little, and trips seemed to take forever before we would arrive. A twenty-minute car ride to see my cousins, which seems to take no time as an adult, felt like hours when I was a child. He is the Creator. It is His timetable, not my own.

It also reminds me of my own kids when they call me at work. It may take me a few hours to get back to them. I often have back-to-back sessions with clients, and I rarely have time to make a call in between the sessions. Just because I didn't answer their call right away doesn't mean I do not love them. I was simply in the middle of something, and I will get back to them as soon as I can. In addition, sometimes I have ulterior motives for not getting back to them. My daughter lived in the dorms in her second semester of college, and she would call me every couple of hours because she hated it. On occasion,

I didn't answer on purpose because I wanted her to get out and meet people rather than talk on the phone with me. I was there for her, but I knew that if she called me ten times a day to complain, she wasn't getting out there and spending time with others. I had my reasons—and they were for her good. She just didn't understand it at the time. But I am wiser than her. She has to trust me.

While I end this chapter with the opinion that it is ultimately our responsibility to make the choices in our lives, I would also argue that it is the responsibility of all of us to make noise for others who are hurting. There is strength in numbers, and the squeaky wheel gets the oil. In closing, take a stand, be bold. Reach out. You may be surprised at who is on the other line, just waiting for you to call. It is also just as likely that the Creator is trying to get your attention, but you just haven't noticed. He may be communicating through other people. Perhaps this book is your call from Him? You had better call back—you only have one more day left!

Heed the warning. You do not want to be infected, or hijacked, never to return home. Worse than thinking there is nothing after this life is the alternative—that there is something far worse out there than this place here on earth. You don't want to be stuck in the jungle somewhere, all alone with your regret, thinking, *If only? If only I had known what I didn't know!*

Self-Reflection Questions

1. Have you ever tried to reach out to the Creator of the universe?

2. If so, when? How often?

3. Have you ever heard back?

4. If you have not tried, why not? What stops you?

5. How would you know if you heard from the Creator of the universe? How would you know His voice?

6. Would you like to have a personal relationship with your Creator? Do you think that is possible? Why or why not?

7. What is something that stood out in the reading?

8. What are some more questions you have?

9. How can you learn more?

10. Now for the "if only" question: What would you have done differently today if you had known you'd be gone in one day?

CHAPTER 11

Go Thrive!

So what? What now? What should you do with all this information, or lack of it? If this book did anything at all, I hope it has actually left you with more questions than when you started. It was meant to do that. This book was meant to leave you with a longing, with a curiosity, with many more questions. Again, I don't have all the answers, but remember: Maybe that's the point. Maybe the point is the search for meaning, the search for truth. Maybe we were left here in the jungle, and our goal is to get out safely on the other side. Maybe it is a kind of school, if you will.

It is hard to navigate all the information out there, all the choices. What makes sense? Keep it simple: Did you ever hear that saying that all you ever needed to learn was in kindergarten? Well, just like that, keep it simple. Look around at the basics. How does nature thrive? That's actually another book. But what does it mean to *thrive*? It means "to grow or to flourish." If we were created and put here, like the trees, like a garden if you planted it, you would want it to grow strong and healthy, because it has purpose and meaning, whether that is to bear fruit, to provide food and nutrients to people, or just to provide beauty for others to love and admire. All living things have purpose and meaning.

Do you have a garden? Do you like to grow things? I don't. I am a terrible plant person. I kill everything green in my path, mostly because I don't have the time to take care of plants. I don't pay attention to the plants or flowers that I have for a myriad of reasons. But what if the simple truth of growing, thriving, and flourishing was just the little things around you? What if it was that simple?

I decided, that while I am not a green thumb for sure, there are basic things that all trees and plants need to flourish. I invite you to take a deeper look at that. But for right now, let's take in the very simple fact that we can learn from everything here on the earth. I often sit and wonder about how, if there evolution really took place, how did each part of creation evolve to be so different? I mean, if the goal of evolution is the survival of the fittest, how did everything get to be so different? For example, if I think of the birds of the sky, how lovely it would be to fly and have the ultimate freedom to escape from one's enemies and to enjoy the scenery from that perspective. I think of the turtle, so slow, but yet able to protect itself with such a hard shell and able to retreat at any time. I think of the gentle deer, so innocent, so vulnerable. Lions, so fierce and so strong. Elephants, so magnificent in their height and weight—and to just think of their trunks, I mean, what is that? The ugly caterpillar that turns into a beautiful butterfly. The ugly water bug that becomes a dragonfly. I'm still not sure about the purpose of alligators or sharks, but wow, just take a few minutes to respect them. If evolution was the cause of everything, wouldn't everything be more of the same? The earth is just crawling with wonder and exciting things to discover every day. And they all have a purpose.

I was thinking of an annoying and ugly vulture the other day as I drove past a mangled rabbit on the side of the road. I looked up at it as it was circling around and around. Well, at least there was something to clean up the mess. We can learn from everything around us. Maybe everything created was for a purpose, to show us things or to be used by us for certain purposes. What can we learn from everything as we look around? I know that isn't a new concept. But take the time to look and really "see" what is around you.

You may be saying to yourself that you do look around and see things. But again, I mean for you to really "see." What do I mean by that? I will admit, I have a really bad and annoying habit. I don't always listen. I mean I "hear," but I don't "listen." For example, anyone who knows me understands that I have a wonderful gift, to be hyper-focused. It is the exact opposite of distractibility. For example, as I sit here writing this, a fistfight could be happening behind me. I might hear it as a distant annoyance, but I am 100 percent immersed in my work. I would not be able to tell you anything about what the fight was actually about. I could continue to work despite so many things.

I used to work as a school psychologist in the middle of stairwell vestibules. I don't know why, but I could still write even as multitudes of students walked right by. I could hear them, for sure, but I didn't listen. It is both a good and a bad quality for me. My husband gets angry with me when I do this. I can't tell you how many times I will be engrossed in work, only for him to tell me he let the dogs out and that he went upstairs. A few minutes later, he would hear me get up and open the door to let them out. I had said "okay" to him. I had heard him with my ears, but I wasn't really, truly listening. I was only processing an audible sound, the physical act of hearing. What I need to do more of is the *mental* part of hearing, the "listening" part. I need to use more of my brain. My ears work fine, but my brain doesn't process what I hear. How many times does that happen to you?

I think it is the same for seeing. Our eyes work fine. I mean, I see the birds, I see the trees, I see nature, but do I really see? Really, truly see? It is not just a physical "eye" thing, but a processing thing. I need to see everything and think about it with my brain. That is the task for today. Just take a few minutes and think about nature around you. Maybe it is given to us, perhaps to provide purpose or to give us direction as a map of some sorts or a blueprint for life. It could be just a simple blueprint put before us that we have eyes to see, but we do not really see. We have ears to hear, but we do not really hear. We have bodies to feel, but we don't want to feel. We avoid feeling, and we avoid uncomfortable emotions. We have emotions, but we don't want to feel. We take prescription drugs, or even street drugs, all in an attempt to avoid our feelings.

Now, I am not talking about everyone. The brain is an organ, and like any organ, sometimes it doesn't work right, and it needs medication to help it stay in balance. But I am talking about the tendency of all of us to avoid feeling negative emotions. We have bodies, but we don't want to feel. Sometimes we numb ourselves because our feelings are too overwhelming. There is so much to think about. Time, of course, is another factor.

Think about how computers were likened after the human brain. Birds were the inspiration for the great airplanes of today. People have looked around and have really seen. Think of Newton, who noticed a simple apple falling and discovered the concept of gravity. Or the great people who got us to the moon because they really looked, more so than a minute of time. They saw, they thought, they discovered. Our brains are amazing. We are amazing creatures. We arrive here an empty slate, but so full of potential. How great it would be if we used our brains for all they were made for. If we used all our senses and explored, asked questions. If we seek, we shall find. You can go through life and just exist. You can have eyes that don't see and ears that don't hear. You can have feelings, but not feel, because it is too much information. But by opening all these things up, we can discover more about ourselves and the world around us. We can make a difference, if not to ourselves, then to others.

It takes curiosity to really open our eyes. What can we learn from the basic blueprint of nature around us? Well, that's for my next book. Like I said, I am no gardener. I will get back to that in my next journey. In the meantime, I am going to explore, open my eyes and ears, learn, and then pass it on to you so you can grow and learn and thrive, as well. Maybe that is the point of it all. I am pushing fifty now. Maybe, if I had done this at age twenty...but better late than never. We don't have much time. I don't have much time. I don't know if I have thirty years left or three days. But I for sure don't want to be the one who says "if only" ever again. Our eternities could depend on it.

GO THRIVE!

Jesus says there will be gnashing of teeth (see Matthew 8:12). To me, that sounds like regret. If only. If only I had used my eyes to see and my ears to hear the truth! You are almost out of time!

Go thrive!

CHAPTER 12

P.S.

I have always been the type of person who will say good-bye, and then say, "WAIT...there's more!" Once again, I think I have done that to you. I had several people read my book, and they wanted to know my faith story. I was not going to share that with you because I wanted you to find your own way, and I didn't want to persuade you in any way with my own story. But after talking with several others, I realized I left the book a little bit on a cliffhanger. And I don't want to leave you hanging. Although I was initially hesitant, I have decided to add this last chapter as a request from others. I am also telling you these things because I realized that not telling you would be similar to someone asking me for directions and me not giving it to them. Again, while I don't want you to think I am telling you what to believe, I do think it's important to tell you how I found my way and why I believe it is the right way. You have the choice to listen to my story and take my directions, my path, or take a different way. The choice is up to you.

P.S.

As a psychologist and a social worker, I am trained to let people make their own decisions, to let them have self-determination. I want to honor that and respect everyone's culture and faith. But I also like to help people. Not telling my story feels a bit like letting you wander in the jungle in the wrong direction toward a path of destruction and danger. My intention of telling you these things is an effort to save you in the future. It is given purely out of love, nothing more. I do want to clarify, I cannot save you, but there is Someone who can, and I don't want to keep that secret all to myself. In my mind, that would be selfish. So, again, it is out of love that I tell you my story. Please take away what you need from it. I do not intend to offend anyone, but I also want to be true to myself and what I believe, and tell you why.

I think I left you hanging at the part of the story where I wrote my pastor in a panic that I didn't believe. I was worried I was going to hell and that I wouldn't see my father again. I really think at that point, it wasn't about God yet; it was more about not seeing my dad ever again.

Well, my pastor, the kind man that he is, told me that it is normal to question your faith. He didn't try to persuade me. He told me to search some more and that I would find Him. By this time in my life, I was smarter, more mature, and more intellectual—or so I thought. I needed some more solid facts. I had lots of questions and objections, I imagine many of the same ones that you think of, such as why were there so many people who wrote the Bible? How do we know they were not just people writing it, rather than inspired by God? Who chose which stories were put in the Bible? Stories change after being told many times. How could they all be true? Seriously, a man being swallowed by a fish? A giant ark that people used to survive a great flood? Some of the stories seemed so silly and unbelievable. Why were there so many inconsistencies? The list of questions went on and on.

To be honest, I have to admit I had these questions and objections, but I looked no further to find the answers. I did not investigate. My pastor's gentle prompting inspired me to search for those answers, and I did. I took a beginner's course for Christians—the Alpha Course. I read *The Case for Christ*. The more I read, the more I wanted to know, and the more it all made sense. All my questions started to be answered—when I looked for the answers. I can't explain it to you, other than if you turn the radio on, you will hear music. I turned the dial on to hear God, and He spoke to me everywhere. I wasn't listening before or seeing. It was like a veil was lifted from my eyes. Oh, trust me, I still struggle with doubts at times, but I trust now that He is smarter than me. Just as my children when they were five didn't understand some things, and I couldn't explain it to them, that is how I think it is with God. There are just some things we humans will never completely understand. We just don't know what we don't know yet. You can't explain the whole world to a five-year-old. And you can't explain the whole universe to human beings. We only can take in small increments of learning and information. But if we do not search or look for the answers, we will never find them.

I promise you, if you tune in to Him, He will respond. But again, you have to search for Him yourself. He knocks, but you have to let Him in. We can be so consumed with our everyday lives and the rat race in which we live that we don't even hear the knock.

One of the best books I ever read that influenced my Christian faith was *The Case for Christ* by Lee Strobel. For those of you who want an intellectual read, it is a good one. The author was an atheist lawyer and journalist who went out on a mission to disprove his wife's faith. He came back with more information that supported the case for Christ. The book is filled with answers to the common questions an atheist might have. Although it is very technical and a bit dry, having been written by a lawyer, it is a fabulous book. For those of you who don't like reading, there is also a movie or documentary about it, as well. But that is not where my story ended, either.

The Alpha Course and *The Case for Christ* were just starters; the real fun began later. Remember what I said:

He reveals Himself to us in small doses. I think God can be too much in one sitting for any person. I have noticed over the years that as time goes by and I experience Him in different ways, my faith grows more and more. But that is only because I search for Him. He is there, if you look. But He shows Himself in small doses of wonder.

In 2015, my family was excited to go on a Disney cruise and to Universal Studios. The girls had been there when they were younger (ages five and three), but they didn't remember much of it. This was the chance for them to experience it all over again. I love to plan vacations. Anyone who knows me knows I am a little on the obsessive side and can tend to overbook myself. If I am in Florida, I want to see everything I can possibly see that week, because I might not be back for many years. This vacation was no different. I found a place near Disney called the Holy Land Experience. The park has replicas from the Holy Land. Since I thought I would probably never get to travel to Israel, I wanted to fit this place in between Disney and Universal, and so we did.

It was a normal sunny, hot day in Florida, and we were making our rounds through the Holy Land Experience. We watched several small theatrical plays of Jesus' life, and we walked from showcase to showcase. As we were walking past one exhibit, we noticed it had a long line. We were heading somewhere else, but the long line attracted our attention. I didn't want us to miss any-

P.S.

thing important. We decided to get in the line, for what I learned later was "the gift." I didn't really know what that meant, but we waited. We finally entered as cattle into the room, to see a replica of the Upper Room where Jesus shared the Last Supper. As we entered, we were instructed to stand in line as a person dressed as Jesus entered the room and started to talk about the gift we would receive. He was talking about the Holy Spirit and how we could receive this gift if we wanted it. He said some of us might start talking in different tongues.

Well, let me stop you right there and explain some things to you. While I was a self-proclaimed Christian at the time, and I certainly thought my faith was pretty solid, I had failed somehow to actually read the entire Bible, specifically the book of Acts. I also had truly failed to grasp the power of the Holy Spirit at the time. Please forgive me for saying this, but it is the truth; when I heard the word "tongues," my brain immediately went to "whackadoos." Images of a church near one of my offices flashed before my eyes. I had been to the church, and nothing unusual had ever happened, but some of my clients told me they had experienced it as being "over the top," with people talking in tongues, falling down, etc.

Ugh, I realized, this was one of those places. As wrong as it was, I immediately went into judgment mode. This was fine for others, but not for me. My thought was that we were in the wrong place, and we needed to leave right away. My oldest daughter looked up at me at that exact moment and said she had to go to the bathroom. Good, I had an excuse to leave! Everything in my being wanted to run out of that room that very moment. But as I looked at her, at the same time, I also had the eerie feeling that something outside of me wanted me to leave. I resisted that being. "Let's just give it a few minutes," I said, and we stayed.

We listened for a few more minutes about a girl who had experienced the Holy Spirit when she was about sixteen years old. I remember her comparing it to a glass of water and putting heat over it. The water would eventually start to boil and overflow, and that is how she explained what would happen to us in the room. Holy Spirit fire would boil up out of us. She also explained that talking in tongues was like talking to God in an unknown, secret language. She said that because it was an unknown language, sometimes we have to trust like babies. She suggested we just start babbling like babies and it would come out of us. She also said that if we did not want the gift, we did not have to take it. God would not force us to take something that we did not want.

So, just a little bit of information before we go further. This whole discussion took no more than five minutes. I was not hypnotized, and I did not drink anything (as my brother thought maybe I did!). However, I do have to stop and digress for just a minute before I go on. Although the experience only lasted a few minutes, there were many thoughts going through my head at the time. One, of course, was that I was in a room with bunch of religious fanatics, but the other thought was a distant memory that was triggered instantaneously.

I told you my father had died of cancer. Well, of course, my mom wanted to try everything before he died, including taking him to a faith healer. My father refused to go. However, I went with her and some friends in hopes that they could pray for my dad's healing. I had totally forgotten about the experience until that very minute, and the memory came rushing back to me. I felt like I was ten years old again. I was in a large stadium, and I believe I was listening to Jimmy Swaggart, or someone like him. I remember everyone vaguely getting filled with the Spirit. I remember standing there looking around at everyone around me. Everyone was feeling something—but I felt nothing. I felt like crying because I felt nothing. I felt left out. I don't think I understood anything about it at the time, other than I wanted it because others had it. What it was, I didn't really know or have the capacity to understand. I don't think my mom felt anything, either. I think I would have remembered her talking more about the Holy Spirit if she had.

For whatever reason, this memory came flooding back, and I had to decide in my head right then and there if I wanted this kooky gift. I thought on it for a second or two. I didn't want to look like some nut, but the feeling of being left out overwhelmed me at that moment. I remember making the conscious decision that I would accept this gift if I had a choice.

The girl directed us to raise our hands in the air. This was hard for me, because even though I love God, I am not an affectionate person in public. Ask my husband. I do not like public displays of affection. I never have. Raising my hands to God is never comfortable for me. I am not sure why. I adore Him. But in my mind, it is a needless public display of affection. It is uncomfortable for my personality. In any case, I half-raised my arms in the air. The girl then instructed us to take baby steps and babble, and the language would come. She also instructed us to say thank You for the gift at the same time in our minds. So, there I was, my hands halfway in the air, babbling baby talk. You really do have to understand how absurd it felt, and I rolled my eyes and said to myself, "This is so stupid."

Then, all of a sudden, out of nowhere, a "force" came over me. That is the only way I know to describe it. This force threw me over into a bowed position, and I almost fell to my knees. Then literally something like vomit started to come out of my mouth. But it wasn't vomit.

P.S.

It was words. I have no idea what I said or what any of the words meant. But it felt as if I had no control. It felt exactly like having a stomach virus and throwing up. I had no control over it. But again, it was words, not vomit, that came rushing out. It was the same feeling, as though something inside of me in my stomach could not contain itself. I was utterly shocked at what was happening. I just couldn't believe it was real. I started laughing and crying at the same time. This was really happening. Snot was running out of my nose, and I did not even care. I literally had been rolling my eyes a moment before. This feeling lasted about a minute or two. I had my eyes closed, but I remember someone putting their hand on my shoulder and saying it was okay. As soon as I heard that person, the feeling whisked away, like a strong wind that had passed. As quickly as it came, it left. I opened my eyes. Next thing you know, they were whisking us out the building like a herd of cattle, on to the next exhibit. The ride was over.

    I had to pull myself to the side. My legs were trembling. There was no conclusion, no explanation. My head was spinning. What the heck had just happened? Again, it was my fault. I didn't know what I didn't know. I didn't truly understand the Holy Spirit. Maybe if I had read more about it, I would have understood. How could I have gone to church all these years and really not have heard about Him. Surely my pastor had talked about it?

But again, I had been listening, but not really hearing, and I'd been seeing with my eyes, but not with my being. But that's a different chapter in my faith story.

Although I had believed in God before that experience, it increased my faith to a new level. I had believed cognitively, but this was a physical feeling beyond anything I had ever experienced before. I was more than 100 percent sure that this was not of this world.

After experiencing all the Universal rides and attractions, such as Dr. Doom's Fearfall and Harry Potter World, I thought I knew what fear, excitement, and magic felt like. The scariest ride of all was the Abyss, which was a waterslide ride we experienced while on our cruise to the Bahamas and during an excursion to Atlantis. The Abyss has a fifty-foot vertical drop into pure darkness. It is the scariest ride I have ever been on in my life. I thought I knew what wobbly legs felt like after that. I think it is interesting of God to pick that moment to show me how much power He has. The excitement, fear, and power of those rides was nothing compared to Him. I was shaking. My world was rocked that day, and I have experienced nothing like it ever again. Trying to get that experience again, I can imagine, is like trying to get that first high. I will likely never match the magic of that day. But of course, it has increased my faith. Even though I always believed with my heart and my mind, it was another thing to feel His "physical" power.

P.S.

The next experience is actually what prompted me to write this book. I woke up talking in tongues one night. Let me back up and explain. For me, the Holy Land Experience definitely increased my curiosity. I began to read and learn everything I could about this odd thing that had happened to me. I probably had about four or five books in my library on the topic of the Holy Spirit. While I have never had the same experience as the first time, I have tried to pray in the Spirit since then. The feeling is never as strong, and I must admit, as sure as I am that first experience was real, I sometimes question my subsequent experiences. I understand the real spiritual gift of tongues is that it is useful for others, and others in the Spirit can interpret what you are saying. However, I have never experienced this. For me, it comes more out of a personal relationship with Him, and it is a very private thing.

But I did have another experience a few years after the first one. I woke up out of sleep talking in tongues. Normally, when I pray, I seek that same experience. I feel like I have always initiated the request. However, this particular evening, the Holy Spirit woke me up out of my sleep, and I awoke talking in tongues. That force was there again, and it seemed so powerful that it was pulling me away. Where to, I simply don't know. I felt pulled somewhere, and then, when I returned, I held on tight to my husband and told him to remember this,

IF ONLY?

then I would be lifted away again. It happened several times, and that is all I remember. I had no real experience of anything other than the vague feeling that I was sitting in front of Jesus and we were talking about a book. I had the sense that I was seeking reassurance that He would help me write this book. My dim recollection is that He kept reassuring me that He would share with me step by step what to do and what to say. Then I woke up. I didn't think that much of it. It must have been a dream, although I couldn't shake the feeling of how odd it was that I was awakened talking in the Spirit, not the other way around.

A few days later, on my Facebook feed there was an ad by Joshua Sprague asking if you ever wanted to write a book. He claimed you could do it in thirty days. I know Facebook has all sort of algorithms and ways to know what I am interested in. But I had not remembered ever searching on anything about how to write a book. It just came to me. I took the course, and what do you know? Out came a book in thirty days. He gave me the step-by-step process of how to do it. I really had not even thought about writing this book. I actually had many other ideas ahead of this particular book. But sparked by the fact that the Feast of Trumpets was in forty days, I decided that this book was a priority. Some people believe the Feast of Trumpets is the dress rehearsal for the Rapture. I thought if I could write one book, this should be it: getting people to think of life if they only had forty days left to live. Of course, this was shortened to ten days, and the rest is history. I do not feel that I wrote it myself. It was too easy. I feel it was inspired by the Creator, by God, or even more specifically, by Jesus.

Again, I cannot tell you what to believe. But that is my story. I believe that He wanted me to share my story with you, so that you would not be lost in this world and suffer from the regret of "if only" you would have known, heard, or seen. I do know He cannot be seen with our naked eyes. But just like radio waves exist, or the speed of light exists, there are many things we cannot see with our eyes. You have to turn the radio on to hear the sounds. You have to turn the switch to see the light. You have to take the first step. You have to search for Him. He is there. Once you start searching, I promise you will see Him, even when you think you can't. He only gives you small doses. He doesn't want to overwhelm you. But He wants you to tune in to Him. He wants you to search for Him and you will find Him. He loves you. He wants you to follow Him. There is so much more He wants to say. If only. If only you would tune in...

Epilogue

"Go to this people and say, 'You will be ever hearing but never understanding; you will be ever seeing but not perceiving.' For this people's heart has become calloused; they hardly hear with their ears and they have closed their eyes. Otherwise they might see with their eyes, hear with their ears, understand with their hearts and turn, and I would heal them."

—Acts 28:26–27

Epilogue

CPSIA information can be obtained
at www.ICGtesting.com
Printed in the USA
BVHW051930070522
636269BV00008B/192